NOW YOU ARE SARA

Now You Are Sara

a memoir

by Caroline Alexander

Translation by John Sandys-Wunsch

Ben-Simon Publications
Port Angeles, Washington
Brentwood Bay, British Columbia

This work is based on the author's memories and impressions. (A version appeared in French in 1992 in *Les Temps Modernes* under the title, "Moi, Poissons-Sagittaire.")

Ben-Simon Publications

USA: P.O. Box 2124
Port Angeles, WA 98362

Canada: P.O. Box 318
Brentwood Bay, B.C. V0S 1A0

Book and jacket design by Rita Edwards
Printed on acid-free paper
Typography by Trade Typesetting, Victoria, B.C.
Published simultaneously in Canada and USA
Printed and bound in Canada by Best Gagné
Acknowledgment to the EHK Memorial Fund

Library of Congress Catalog Number: 93-072361

Canadian Cataloging in Publication Data:
Alexander, Caroline, 1936-
Now You Are Sara
ISBN 0-914539-07-8
1. Alexander, Caroline, 1936- –Journeys–Germany–Mönchengladbach. 2. Reunions–Germany–Möonchengladbach. 3. Refugees, Jewish–Belgium–Biography. 4. Women, Jewish–Germany–Biography. 5. Holocaust, Jewish (1939-1045)–Germany.
I. Title.
DS135.G5A44 1993 943'.553'004924 C93-091605-0

to my mother,
my husband,
to those I love.

Preface

Caroline Alexander's story is nothing if not a tour de force about the most devastating events of this often devastating century. With neither self-pity nor vengeance she paints herself intimately into the tragedy of the Jews of one German town. And she takes us with her, at whirlwind speed, back and forth, between the Paris of 1964 and Mönchengladbach near the end of the 1980s. At first we think we have opened a fanciful personal memoir. A young woman in Paris is in love. Twenty-five years later she comes as a mature but apprehensive visitor to the German town of her birth. Mystic encounters in Paris give way to quizzical ones in Mönchengladbach. But that is surface. Just below we encounter Holocaust and aftermath.

The City of Mönchengladbach had invited all its once-upon-a-time Jewish citizens, all the survivors who could be located, for a reunion. In it the Ruhr-Rhine city was following what some other towns, cities, and villages in the old Federal Republic of Germany had begun the year before: to commemorate the 50th anniversary of the pogrom of November 9-10, 1938. Nazi propaganda had misnamed it *Kristallnacht*, "the night of broken glass"; in reality it was a state-orchestrated systematic destruction of Jewish houses of prayer, Jewish homes, and Jewish lives. All the earlier acts of discrimination and planned terror, from 1933 on, had been mere foretastes. The pogrom of November 1938 served as the signal for the start of Hitler's "Final Solution"– extermination.

Like this book's author, I had come to Mönchengladbach for the 1989 reunion. One hundred and sixty-four returnees plus companions–mostly spouses, friends, or grown children–were billeted in four hotels in different parts of the city. At night, after meetings or entertainments, buses would bring us back to our temporary abodes. Thus in the evenings and at breakfasts we met mainly people who shared our particular hotel. Caroline Alexander and her "little mother" were staying elsewhere and, not having known each other before, we met only by chance once or twice during the "reunion." Weeks later, in Paris, we met Caroline again and talked at length.

In Paris Caroline told us about her planned "memoir" and that she wanted us to consider it for publication. She would send French and English versions to us in Canada. Early in 1990, that conversation all but forgotten, the promised manuscripts arrived. Deeply moved by them, we told Caroline that, after previous commitments had been met, we would publish her. But when she suggested I write a preface to the coming English edition, I demurred. Reading her work and finding it gripping I doubted whether a preface was needed.

What in the end made me write a preface was the difference in our childhood pictures. In contrast with Caroline's, mine was pallid and so could only highlight hers. Unlike Caroline, I had lived in Mönchengladbach to age sixteen. In the spring of 1934, a little more than a year after Hitler had come to power, having completed six years of "Gymnasium," the classical high school, I transferred to a school in England. I was far more fortunate than many other young people who could not leave Germany so early, or not at all. And I was fortunate in yet another way: among the returnees of 1989 many had lost members of their immediate family; I had not. But that week in Mönchengladbach I was my family's only representative. My brothers had declined the city's invitation and our parents were long dead.

Whatever those who invited us might have had in mind, most of us came with our own agenda. Mine was that of a scholar who, for obvious reasons, had studied the impact of catastrophic events on human lives. But my work had not directly dealt with the dissolution of Jewish existence in

Germany. In the winter of 1988 I received a letter of invitation from my former hometown. It was the brainchild of Dr. Günter Erckens and the Society for Christian-Jewish Cooperation. Erckens, the Mönchengladbach lawyer, having some years earlier contacted me about my family's history, had written a two-volume chronicle on Jewish life in the area, spanning six centuries. The strain of the work had apparently affected his health: shortly before his dream of a reunion could be realized he died. Now the Society for Christian-Jewish Cooperation was sponsoring the reunion and the City was footing the bill.

In accepting the city's invitation I did so without expectation of reconciliation. I would come to Mönchengladbach largely for my parents' sake. Their lives had been much more badly disrupted than mine. Dead, they could not speak for themselves. Still, I had misgivings. Reading and re-reading the letter of invitation and the proposed agenda for the reunion week, I thought back to many of my classmates at the Gymnasium and to our neighbors in town. With the Nazi wind blowing hard in everyone's face, many had distanced themselves from us, first imperceptibly and then openly, without shame. But I also remembered how, just as I was getting ready to leave for school in England, one of the boys in my class whom I had known only by sight and name, the red-haired Herbert Stienecke, had come to our house to say good-bye. That small but not unimportant gesture had become an anchor for what little has remained of my sense of being a *German* Jew. On my first return to Europe in 1965, I went briefly to Mönchen-gladbach and searched the records of former Gymnasium teachers and classmates. Herbert Stienecke had been killed at the Russian front.

Some months before the 1989 journey to Mönchengladbach I had been asked by a teacher in one of its high schools to correspond with his eleventh-graders. Knowing my German long in disrepair, I accepted with trepidation. Five weeks were spent, dictionary at elbow, writing letters about the years of my childhood in the city then called M.Gladbach. After several such letters I felt myself on firmer linguistic ground and perhaps also readier, emotionally, for the encounters to come. My wife is an American; she has only a bit of school-German, and though Jewish, does not have my ingrained love-hate connection with Germany and things German. In the summer of 1989, preparing for our trip, I thought it might be helpful if she heard some German spoken before we got to Mönchengladbach. The subjects of the mealtime "discourses" were not confined to domestic matters. One day I mentioned some of those non-verbal behavior signs that anyone with first-hand experience of Nazi antisemitism will probably recognize. I said, "when we walk through Mönchengladbach streets you may notice some older people looking at me with undisguised displeasure." I had avoided the word "hate" so that Beve would not at once think of paranoia. She nevertheless expressed her doubts and we left the matter at that.

After the second day in the "old hometown," perhaps having forgotten my warning about non-verbal behavior in "Nazi-German," she said, "I noticed some people in the street giving you funny looks." Then, with sudden recall, she laughed the laugh of recognition. It helped her see the reality back of my "paranoia," and gave us both an inkling of what lay behind Jean Amery's ingeniously sad reference to Nazi Germany as the *Feindheimat*, the enmity-homeland.

In Caroline Alexander's story you will come upon an event that the Mönchengladbach city fathers meant as a special treat for us: a gala excursion on an elegant Rhine steamer. With my "paranoia" I could not avoid thinking of the passage of the *S.S. St. Louis*, made infamous by the film "Journey of the Damned." At the hotel breakfast I had mentioned it. Beve had given me a disapproving look: why was I spoiling things? A couple of hours later we were at the dock in Bonn. Moving onto the gang-plank we both heard a man in front of us say loudly: "There you have it, the *St. Louis.*" It was in the air.

As the young woman in love in Paris, and later as the mature visitor to Mönchengladbach, Caroline Alexander has given voice to mute feelings. This footbridge of hers leads over an unfathomable chasm, a terrible past. It cannot be plumbed with reason; perhaps, in the nature of things, it is not understandable. Yet with eyes for invisibles and ears for things inaudible, we can recognize in this work sights and sounds of Greek drama and the Book of Job.

H. David Kirk (Heinz Kirchheimer), 1993

Translator's Note

This work is the voice of one woman speaking. In reflecting out loud on an intersection of past and present in her life produced by a visit to the town of her birth, discovery and catharsis together help her transmute experience into art.... As in poetry, meaning comes from richness of allusion and a deliberate juxtaposition of varied images without any attempt made at logical transitions.

In this translation I have tried to cope with two problems. The first difficulty is preserving the "chunkiness" of the style to allow meaning to seep out between the cracks in the logical structure. The second difficulty is deciding how far can one depart from the original text in order to give the occasional hint to North American readers who are not as a group immersed in the French intellectual European culture of the author.

John Sandys-Wunsch, March 1993.

Medieval cities, like secular and ecclesiastic princes, identified themselves by escutcheons. Such crests typically depict what probably derives from their history or myth. Caroline Alexander's narrative is built around two cities: Paris, French metropolis, and Mönchengladbach, provincial West German city. Their crests will serve her story as way-markers.

Crests were sometimes redrawn and altered in content and style. Here an artist's rendering depicts Paris and Mönchengladbach crests as they were half a century ago, just before and during World War II. It is the era of our author's infancy and early childhood. Any connection between the crests' images and Caroline Alexander's story are of course accidental. Yet in each there is a hint of themes related to *Now You Are Sara.*

Paris (left) has at its center a sailing ship surmounted by a crown made up of parapets in the wall of the old city. The ship seems a link to our story, for our child-author has to flee and finds refuge in the walls of a French-speaking city. The crest's Latin motto, here omitted, says *FLUCTUAT NEC MERGITUR*: freely translated as "she rides the bounding waves, but will not sink".

Mönchengladbach (right) has at its center the figure of a child, surrounded by stars. It is the *Findelkind*, the legendary foundling-patron of the city. Caroline Alexander is the archetypal foundling. Even the stars have a part to play.

I was born on a 25th of February. Under the sign of Pisces say the horoscopes, a sign of water. But I had to wait half a century to know the sign of my ascendant, that sign which is calculated from the hour of birth. I had the day, but not the hour. I have just learned it, finally: I was born at 3 a.m. One of my friends consulted a manual: my ascendant is the sign of Sagittarius, a sign of fire. Water and fire ...

I never read horoscopes, not even at the hairdresser's. But I do find astrology has its uses; it's a good subject for conversation. "What's your sign? Oh, really ... and your ascendant? You don't say, I really thought that ..."

Astrology for conviviality, for exchanging confidences, for breaking down barriers, for disarming people ... On one occasion, a long time ago, in 1964–summertime, I will always remember it–a strange little man consumed by a passion for esoteric knowledge wanted to find out all sorts of things for me from my astrological data. Since I wasn't able to supply him with the hour of my birth, he found himself with a difficult problem on his hands, but he nonetheless took a lot of trouble to do many calculations. Finally he told me that in my stars there had been a "sacrificed" home from the time I was very small, something like a loss beyond recovery or a disappearance forever ... he took great pains to discover all this, without knowing the hour of my birth, without being able to determine my ascendant....

I was born on a 25th of February, 1936, the year of the Popular Front in France, of Léon Blum and the first paid-holidays, a year of hope. But not for me. I was born in a place where the word "hope" was not permitted. In Mönchengladbach, "glittering brook of the monks," in the German Rhineland. There the government had been National-Socialist for the past three years and its racial laws were taken very seriously. I was born in Mönchengladbach at 3 a.m. between the old marketplace and the abbey. But not in a clinic; the local clinics were off-limits.... I was born on the second floor of number 10A, Gasthausstrasse, the street of inns, the street that welcomes you, the street of whores and cathouses. "Next to a house of ill-repute, a brothel?" said an old lady.... "No, right above a brothel," said an old man who had known my father. No one was sure; the memory of the events surrounding my birth was unclear. It had been a long time since those who heard my first cries had fallen silent. One thing was sure in 1936, in Mönchengladbach Jews no longer had the right to live in the nice parts of town and their wives were not allowed to give birth in the hospitals, so in that year little Jewish girls were born near brothels. Did it make sense for a baby to be born near brothels in 1936? Did it make sense for a Jewish baby to be born at all in Mönchengladbach in 1936?

Mönchengladbach, August 1989

"Number 10A Gasthausstrasse is still standing." The officer in charge of security in the city of Mönchengladbach slips a memo onto the note-pad where I am writing down some figures about the town's economic development since 1980. I am seated at a large table in the town hall's council chamber. Opposite me, "the director of the town hall"—in effect the number-two man of the town, a sort of deputy mayor—along with the council members, is responding to questions put by a handful of very special visitors.

In another time these visitors had been ordinary citizens of Mönchengladbach, of Rheydt, of Odenkirchen.... Today they live in Buenos Aires, Sydney, New York, Bogotá, London, Toronto, Paris, Los Angeles, Vancouver. They speak German, their mother tongue, with the music of the accents of their adopted countries. They all had mothers, brothers, cousins, friends, neighbors, grandparents who died in the smoke and the pits of Auschwitz, of Riga, and elsewhere. These visitors here had been able to flee and escape in time from the Holocaust. These are some of the survivors. I am one of them.

The town of Mönchengladbach had invited us to go back to our old roots and intertwine them with our new ones. A pilgrimage. I am in my native town that I had left secretly at the age of three with a large woollen cap pulled down over my head to hide my black hair, with strict orders to keep my eyes closed and to say nothing during the journey in the train. On pain of a terrible punishment–they had warned me–for there was danger of death! The "Aryan" friend who had saved me remembers: "You were so good and quiet; you huddled up under my coat, you pretended to sleep in my arms during the whole journey, you understood, you knew the danger." Myself, I have no memories of it at all. Here in Mönchengladbach, will I at last be able to recreate them? Who will tell me where I lived? At what time of day was I born?

Paris, June 1964

Evening tints the fronts of the buildings with a golden glow just before night falls. Lovers walk for hours to savor the glow of the evening. I was young and newly married and we loved the movies. In the Boulevard de Sébastapol, close to the Antoine Theater we had just discovered, in a cinema without air conditioning, *Pierrot le Fou* (Pierrot the Fool). Ah, Godard! We were living near the Place de la Bastille, fifth floor up with a stairwell facing the inner courtyard, five hundred square feet, view of the gray and pink roofs with, in good weather, an outlook on the hills of Meudon shaped like a row of dark nipples.

We decide to return on foot to prolong the shock of this film which was thumbing its nose at the rules of the seventh French art, the cinema, and to discuss the "New Wave." Tender quibbling interrupted with laughs and kisses. We go on holding each other tight, Boulevard du Temple, Boulevard Saint-Martin, the theaters, the Renaissance, the Saint Martin gate, and the Ambigu Theater which was living out its last moments at the entry to the Rue René-Boulanger, the Ambigu with its tiny book and stationery store cut out of its sides.

"Is the rumor true about the Ambigu going to be pulled down?" asks the tall, thin boy with whom I had agreed to share my life. I tell him about the theater's bankruptcy, about the indifference of the Minister of Culture who was playing Pontius Pilate in the face of urbanization, about useless petitions ... 'even Michel Simon has signed.' But all to no effect. The decision was taken, the theater was to be razed and in its place there would be a garage, some offices, or a supermarket. The "Boulevard of Crime" named for the tumult of the low-brow and rowdy theater district, made famous by Marcel Carné's 1940s film *Les Enfants du Paradis* (Children of Paradise), would never be the same again. "And what about that?" Maxime nods toward the little bookshop. With a wave of my hand, I say, "Same thing!"

On the sidewalk a revolving stand of postcards is attracting idlers. The cards are very old and in lamentable taste–the Eiffel Tower in the Champ de Mars with crudely colored tulips, the Moulin Rouge, the Arc de Triomphe. "Souvenirs of Paris"... and absurdly lost in the middle of them all St. Theresa of Lisieux with a halo of gold spangles on permed hair. It's so absurd that I want it. "How much is the portrait of St. Theresa, monsieur?"

We have entered the store which smells of dust and garlic sausage. Behind his counter the owner is wearing an apothecary's cap and a long gray smock. He doesn't reply. He serves a tourist who hands him three "Palaces of Versailles" and a reproduction of Utrillo's "Hill of Montmartre." "For St. Theresa?" I offer my coin. The proprietor rubs his hands on his smock and disappears without saying a word behind a sort of glass partition at the back of his shop.

Music suddenly breaks forth—Wagner—sumptuous. "The Prelude to *Tristan*," Maxime whispers, his head tilted back to see the highest shelf of the philosophy section before taking down some book by Kant or Spinoza.

The proprietor still doesn't take my money. He looks at my postcard through his small greasy glasses. "Look, this isn't really the portrait of St. Theresa, mademoiselle, this is only some person posing for a photographer." He's shocked; he had pronounced the word "person" like an epithet. "She doesn't even look like her." Is he going to make me scream with impatience or only laugh? Must I tell him that I am buying his postcard only because I find it funny and that I care as much about the face of St. Theresa as I do about the face of Louis XVI?

I look for Maxime's reaction, but he's already engrossed in his reading. "Oh yes?" I didn't find anything else to say; I tug at my husband's sleeve to get his help. The proprietor is looking at me with his small eyes distorted by the lenses of his glasses, his finger pointed in the air. "It's beautiful,..." Maxime, my husband, my goy, my challenge goes further, "Yes,... the opera whose love-potion makes you crazy—*Tristan*, one of the most beautiful." The proprietor ignores his comments, doesn't see him, doesn't listen to him.

"You know, you look like her a little. There, around the jaws, you have an obstinate look,..." He puts his hand out towards my face and I recoil; he makes motions in the air and confides to me *mezza voce*, as one confides a secret, that St. Theresa had the jaw of a leader. "And a look that was at the same time idealistic and thoughtful. I have studied her astrological portrait, mademoiselle. What you see there on that postcard is neither the color of her hair, nor the shape of her nose, nor her mouth. Our faces are written in the stars. Mine, yours ... I have spent years studying the astrological chart of St. Theresa. I know everything about her. I will show you. Just let me serve this gentleman."

Mönchengladbach, August, 1989

The press officer of the mayor of Mönchengladbach, has organized the trips and the accommodation of the guests. A year of work. She is smiling, patient, tired. She will be relieved once the Jews have left ... She doesn't admit it, but I can guess, I understand. It's an explosive situation with these wounded visitors, so very sad ...

"I would like to reimburse you for your travel expenses," she tells me. "For cars we pay by the number of kilometers covered." But there is a problem; there are two rates, thirty-one pfennigs for the support staff and thirty-eight for the administrators. The rules say nothing about the guests. "It will be the administrators' rate, obviously," says the press officer to her assistant who calls the accounting office right away. "What? Thirty-one pfennigs? The rate for support staff? But it's for one of our guests; she comes from Paris. Hello, do you hear me?" He begins to speak in a low voice; he turns red. I turn away from him and occupy myself in reading the prospectus. "Thirty-one pfennigs, OK, I understand."

The assistant is red-faced; he attempts to smile. "How many kilometers should I put down?"

The press officer hurries; she has to get on to something else and forget the affront of thirty-one pfennigs given by the accounting office. "I have been looking into your birth certificate. Our registers may perhaps have recorded the address and the time. While we are getting your expense check ready, why not go along to Dr. Schmidt; he's our liaison with the city administration."

We make our way through the long corridors briskly. Sand-colored carpets, panelled walls. I would have liked to have heard the accountant's reply, I would have liked to have seen his face when he snapped at the assistant that for me the rate for support staff was adequate. What had he said exactly that had made the young assistant blush? I felt sorry for the assistant and sorry for the press officer.

Paris, June 1964

In the Ambigu's bookstore, the tourist has pocketed the change from his three "Palaces of Versailles" and the "Hill of Montmartre." The owner adjusts his cap and his gray smock and bending down brings out a shoebox hidden underneath the counter. "Everything about St. Theresa is here," he tells me unrolling a sort of astrological chart studded with planets and signs of the zodiac. "Theresa of the baby Jesus ... born Alençon in the Orne, January 2, 1873 at 11:30 p.m., died at Carmel de Lisieux in 1897, beatified in 1923, canonized in 1925 by Pius X! ... You can see, mademoiselle, she had to wait fully twenty-eight years before the church gave her her due." He was clearly expecting me to approve of his indignation. "Really ..."

I try one last time to get him to take my coin; I want to do what the tourist had done, pay for my postcard and go. I am impatient; all of a sudden I am full of ideas about *Pierrot le Fou* and I want to share them with Maxime. I share everything with him. I love him.

"She had very straight eyebrows ... like her nose. Her mouth was also straight, generous, never pinched ... no sign of greed ... you understand me, mademoiselle?" I should have replied "Yes, yes, of course, quite right," and then I would have been free of that man in the gray smock, but I fell into the trap, head first. "Uh,... yes,... no,... not really." "I will explain it to you then; you will see how simple it is." He spreads out a second chart.

A small boy has just come into the bookstore; he's nine or ten years old and wears a yarmulke on his wavy hair. He's sweet. I wonder if one day I will have a little boy like that one ... Maxime is not Jewish, our little boy will certainly not wear a yarmulke and yet he will be my little Jew for me, his Jewish mother ... The little boy looks along the shelf of comic books; there is not much there, a few *Tintins,* some *Spirou, Pieds Nickelés,* and *Bécassine.* "Do you have *Flight 714 for Sydney*?" the boy asks the proprietor. "We are closed." The tone is surprisingly harsh. Maxime looks up from his book, he notices the little boy, who, surprised and blushing as if he had been caught doing something wrong, points at the shelf of comic books. He opens his mouth to ask a question. "Closed," the proprietor says again. Maxime shuts his book of philosophy and puts it back on the high shelf where it had slept in oblivion, and then bends over to investigate the shelf of comic books.

The little boy goes out of the shop in silence. On the sidewalk he turns around a couple of times beside the revolving postcard rack. Maxime waves *Flight 714 for Sydney,* the little boy looks at him in a puzzled way and goes off looking backwards.

Maxime grasps my hand and squeezes it hard. A message. Don't show any surprise, don't say anything. I understand. During that year of 1964 we do not need to speak to understand each other. Theresa of Lisieux and her strange astrologer are beginning to interest us.

Mönchengladbach, August, 1989

The press officer takes me back into the council chamber. The deputy mayor winks at me; he rather likes me. He is the one who undertakes the business of finding out my hour of birth and where I was born. "Here we can find everything. We are well organized, you know." By good luck it turns out that the town hall had not been bombed, the archives are pretty well intact. "We will certainly find the address, that's no problem. Finding the hour of birth will depend on the place: if it was in a hospital there is no difficulty, but if it was at home ... In those days, nothing was simple ..."

In those days not everyone was allowed into hospital. I don't yet understand what the deputy mayor is trying to say. The professor from Vancouver takes notes on the problems of education for Turkish immigrants, a lady from Luxembourg asks questions about drugs. I am only half listening. I hear myself ask a question, "What was the percentage of Jews among the more successful businessmen in 1933?" The person in charge of economic affairs clears his throat. "More than 65% I believe ... It's very painful for us to say so." Painful for them! Poor dears ... And for us?

A messenger has just entered; he holds out a little envelope to the deputy mayor who looks at it, smiles with satisfaction, and brings it over to me. My heart stops–for a moment. "But it is an official identification card like the one I already have. It is not my birth certificate." So much the worse, I am stuck with my mystery. "What time were you born, my dear?" "Shsssh–I think it's a state secret!"

Paris June 1964

It's still daylight on the sidewalk by the Ambigu. The little boy has been stopped by a cyclist who is asking him all sorts of questions about the theater. The boy shakes his head, he doesn't know, he points towards the bookstore and shrugs his shoulders in a discouraged way. The proprietor hasn't seen this. He is in the middle of his astrological chart of St. Theresa: "... the conjunction Sun/Saturn was forming in Capricorn in the fourth House ... you follow, mademoiselle?..." He asks the question without raising his head.

I pass the time by looking at the cyclist who tries to lean his bicycle against the rack of postcards. The rack falls—crash!—the postcards tumble into the gutter. The cyclist picks up the rack and in his confusion the bicycle falls on its side, its wheels spinning in the air ... This makes quite a din in the heat of the June summer evening. The little boy comes back and helps the cyclist gather up the cards. I am not sure if I feel like laughing. I hear, in the distance, the proprietor recite: "It's so simple ... The hour of birth of St. Theresa shows us that her ascendant was Libra with the Moon in Pisces and Venus in Aquarius ..."

My hands are damp in Maxime's grip. Why had I married him? The cyclist has just leaned his bike carefully against the shop window. The little boy has gone. Why had I got myself into the rut of a bourgeois marriage? I did not want it ... All my life—I had always dreamt of living by myself in a traveling performer's catch-all garret, stuffed full of all kinds of things accessible only to me, in the midst of a large house full of friends and lovers.

I had felt an obligation to my little adoptive mother and the father who had replaced my real one without asking anything in return. Because of this feeling, I fell into step and stood in before the mayor instead of a rabbi ... One had to make allowance for my choice of this impoverished fiancé with the looks of a Viking, who had nothing, absolutely nothing in common with what used to be called a "good match"...

In 1964, in the month of June, I was happy and triumphant; he was destined for me I was sure ...

"Excuse me I am looking for *La Reine Verte*, I believed it was playing at the Ambigu, but ..." The cyclist had come into the bookstore, he has a blue cap and an iron-gray mustache, and carries a schoolboy's satchel. He's sweating.

"It is closed," says Maxime, imitating the proprietor's voice.

"Closed?" replies the cyclist astounded, "no performance today?"

"Closed forever," I add and I explain to this cyclist lover of theater the sad fate awaiting one of the most beautiful stages of Paris. He's not upset.

"But *La Reine Verte* ...," in a worried voice.

"At the Hébertot Theater, Boulevard des Batignolles, do you know it?"

"I knew Hébertot, is he still alive? Look, he signed his autograph for me ten years ago and I thought ... He was old then, but he looked good."

Beneath his black skullcap the proprietor sees nothing, hears nothing of what is going on in his shop. The Prelude to *Tristan* finishes. All of a sudden our voices fill the room; without the music we are speaking too high. The owner precipitously leaves his astrological chart of St. Theresa and disappears behind the glass partition.

In a normal voice Maxime suggests the cyclist should hurry up, "you have missed the opening, but if you get going on your bike you may make it in time for the second half."

"But you don't understand, I don't care about the play ... it's the intermissions that interest me ... obviously ..."

We don't hear the end of his sentence. A crash of thunder, it's the "Ride of the Valkyries" which comes down on our heads–boom! boom!–the sound is cranked up as far as it will go, we can hear nothing more. Maxime shouts, "Intermissions?" The owner notices us from behind his glass wall; he disappears again, the Valkyries still ride their steeds, but at a distance.

The cyclist brings out a large black notebook from his satchel. "Of course, intermissions ... It has to do with my collection ..."

Mönchengladbach, August, 1989

They had managed to track down one hundred and eighty former citizens spread throughout the world. A tour de force made possible by the publication of a definitive work, *Juden in Mönchengladbach* (Jews in Mönchengladbach), by Günter Erckens, two volumes of painstaking research retracing the odyssey of Jewry in the region from the Middle Ages to the Holocaust. Erckens, who had died in 1988 several months after his retirement as a senior civil servant in the finance ministry, was an amateur historian devoted to local history. He had written several books on the history of his hometown and its surrounding areas.

Juden in Mönchengladbach had taken ten years of work. He wanted to know everything, family by family. He got in touch with the brothers, the children, the cousins of those who had disappeared along with those few who had survived the camps. He listened to them and wrote it all down. It was an inter-religious group, the Society for Christian-Jewish Cooperation (Gesellschaft für Christlich-Jüdische Zusammenarbeit) that had suggested the municipality bring together once more all the survivors and those who had been able to flee in time.

Letters of invitation were sent out and advertisements

published in newspapers. Result: one hundred and sixty-four souls from the diaspora of Mönchengladbach replied "present" and made the trip. Average age: seventy-three, an average fortunately lowered by their younger companions! "Some of those contacted declined our offer because of health reasons," the press officer informed me. "Only one wrote she would never set foot here again." Cost of the operation: one million marks given by the city, one hundred and fifty thousand marks collected from various firms. The pious hope: that the whole region would take part in the welcome for these living shadows from the past—a hope in part fulfilled by the hotels, the schools, the florists, the cultural and religious institutions, etc. One great fear: that those citizens with a taste for "nostalgia" might show their incurable antisemitism.

No decoration or banners of welcome in the streets ... "Imagine the disgrace if some s.o.b. decided to tear them down!" The s.o.b.'s didn't show themselves, and yet they do exist. In order for the visitors to meditate in the two Jewish cemeteries, they had to ask for the key from a survivor of Auschwitz, Manfred, my cousin. Deported at the age of eight with a thousand other children of whom he is the sole survivor, Manfred who has never spoken about it.

He is the keeper of the cemeteries. He returned to live in his native land to maintain the ruined graves. "I am obliged to double-lock the gates, you understand. There have been so many desecrations since the war's end. Now that we've managed to tidy things up thanks to a grant and volunteer work on the part of a group of high school students, we have to be even *more* vigilant."

On the subject of this grant, an opposition member who was a candidate in the local municipal elections remarked in a local paper: "Why this grant at the taxpayers' expense? Traditionally in cemeteries it is the families of the dead who take care of the upkeep of the vaults and gravestones." He did not reply to those who asked him the reason why, pray, the families of the dead in the Jewish cemeteries of Mönchengladbach were so negligent ...

Yes, "the womb is still fertile from which the foul brute came,..." it's not I but they who here summon Bertolt Brecht.

The mayor cried during his welcoming speech. He suddenly remembered the beautiful synagogue burning to the cheers and shouts of the crowd during the *Kristallnacht*. He was twelve years old on the tenth of November, 1938. His mother had brought him deliberately to see it all. "Look, look at what they are doing, and never forget!" She did not like the Nazis. Her son, having become His Honor the Mayor, had not forgotten. He is ashamed, they are all ashamed, all those who had feverishly prepared the visit of these hundred and sixty-four relatives and cousins of the ghosts who stalk them in the nights and the mists.

Paris, June 1964

"You collect intermissions?" In the Ambigu's bookstore that was being pounded by the boots of the Valkyries, the owner in his gray smock has come up to us. With a distracted air he gives the impression of having just discovered us. "Gentlemen ...!" he speaks to the cyclist and Maxime.

"Not intermissions, no, nothing of that sort!" the cyclist exclaims. "Autographs! I have two thousand ... In here!" He takes a black notebook out of his satchel. He turns to the bookseller: "Sorry to bother you; I am not a customer, I just came in to ask for some information and this young couple has been kind enough to give it to me. I am looking for Maria

Casarès. I thought she was at the Ambigu. But no, she's not there; it appears she's at the Boulevard des Batignolles. For the intermission it's a bit late; so I will knock on her dressing room door after the performance ... I missed her once before when she was at the Odéon; this time I hope ..."

"Autograph hunter," mutters the bookseller going back to his counter and the astrological charts of St. Theresa. He's thoughtful under his skullcap. He coughs to get my attention. "Take a look at this, mademoiselle, our Theresa's mother, Amélie Martin, was also a Capricorn with Libra in the ascendant; Theresa's father, Louis Martin, was Leo with Virgo in the ascendant ..."

Maxime is enjoying the evening's chance happenings; an action film, a tacky postcard, a bookseller hooked on astrology and mad about Wagner, a Jewish boy who lets himself be sent away and now an eccentric cyclist who collects autographs.

I scarcely pay any attention to the bookseller reciting his astrological litany. The cyclist laughs, wipes his brow. "If you only knew how much I hurried! I'm sweating. I rode my bike so hard ... I live a long way off, you know, and I cannot come just anytime I want. I'm a mailman at Alençon; I collect autographs and, once in a while, I play the cello in the municipal orchestra."

I listen to Maxime. "You have two thousand autographs from actors?" The cyclist shakes his head and frowns. "I only get autographs from great people; there aren't two thousand geniuses in the theater or the films. I can show you; there is Louis Jouvet and there Charles Dullin." He leafs through his note book quickly as if it were a telephone directory. "There is Arletty ... here is Pierre Fresnay, Marie Bell, Jean Marais, Jacques Copeau.... That one gets you, doesn't it, Jacques Copeau!" I ask him who are his favorites. "The poets ..." Maxime wants to know if he has met many of these, for in his opinion poets are a bit unsociable.

The bookseller's voice has stopped in the middle of a sentence, "... mother dead from cancer when Theresa was five years old. The Moon moves into Saturn, death ..." Or is it just that I am no longer listening? The cyclist seems familiar. He looks like someone who came to see us from time to time, my little mother and me in the apartment on the Rue des Sicambres in Brussels where we were hiding. He used to come to bring us some potatoes, a cauliflower or beets, and once a month an egg ... He often spoke of God and of a very nice person whom I did not know, the baby Jesus. He spoke so highly of this child that I began to love him and at nights I used to dream that the ban was finally lifted, the ban forbidding me to go into the Rue des Sicambres, that blind alley by the railway, and that the two of us, the baby Jesus and I, played hopscotch.

The German soldiers never noticed us; they were always too caught up in questioning the watchmaker on the corner, a nasty man with little round glasses who always wore a gray shirt and an apothecary's skullcap on his head. I learned later, after my war, that the watchmaker was a collaborator ... The cyclist was a priest in mufti who was part of the Resistance ... a Benedictine monk, Father Bruno Reynders. Leaving his cassock hanging in the vestry in the abbey of Ottignies, he saved 390 Jewish children. He had many names, all of them false. After his death he was given a true one: "Hero of the Resistance and Righteous among the Nations."

Now the cyclist goes through his notebook solemnly. He is proud: "Jean Cocteau ... Jacques et Pierre Prévert ... René Char ... Jean Paulhan–I had to wait three hours for him! In front of his office door. He was so nice, genuinely nice, and quite astonished that I was interested in him. He put a dedication to me above his signature ... Look, I am going to photograph this page and frame it ..."

The bookseller finally stops talking; he has gone behind his glass partition again. New phonograph record, same sound level; we are now treated to the Overture to *Tannhäuser*.

"Oh, that one," jokes the cyclist. He puts two fingers over his upper lip and parodies the Nazi salute. "On that, ladies and gentlemen, if I am not going to miss Maria Casarès, I will have to be going. Thanks for everything and have a good evening."

On the threshold of the door he stops, points in the air as if indicating the music, and then gives it "the finger." He picks up his bike that has stayed put against the shop window, mounts it and disappears among the cars. It's 10 p.m. We are still in the Ambigu's bookstore and evening has finally thrown its shadow on the pavement.

Mönchengladbach, August, 1989

In the town hall's council chamber, I put my official identification card in my purse, I try to listen to the discussion. The subject gets onto sport and inevitably onto soccer–the Mönchengladbach team plays at the international level–someone mumbles about the matches played against Israel–"unfortunately we always win,"–the deputy mayor seems to have taken a fancy to me, whispers several words into the ear of his neighbor Dr. Marcus Antonius, the official in charge of order and security.

Dr. Marcus Antonius leaves the room. He returns in ten minutes, comes straight over to me and says in a hushed tone, "three a.m., 10A Gasthausstrasse." My pulse leaps. I make him repeat the precious information word by word. Quick, note it down correctly! 3 a.m. I was certain that I was born during the night ... I would never have been born at 3 p.m., never. I love the night. I love the dawn and the long summer evenings. I have never liked the afternoon!...

Herr Marcus Antonius leans over towards me; he has just had an idea, he glows with pleasure. "Would you like a photocopy?" And how! A certainty, black on white, concrete, a piece of paper to hold onto and read time and time again.

Marcus Antonius goes off again. He is proud to do a favor for the little Jewish woman. They would all like to do us favors, they would like to be helpful. I suppose that that would assuage them, it's very human, too human ... What are they talking about now? Soccer? Still soccer?

I could ask a question about sports in school, facilities for the handicapped, or about anything else just to change the subject, to show that I am good little journalist, a professional who never misses anything. But no, I daydream. It is 3 a.m., there is hoarfrost on the windows of number 10A, Gasthausstrasse. A woman on a large, messed-up bed holds, smilingly, a red-faced and howling newborn. "It's a girl!" There is flowered wallpaper on the walls, a crack in the ceiling looks like a teapot. The baby is held with its head down. The umbilical cord is not yet cut. "Come and see your little sister, my boy, but don't touch." The room smells of disinfectant and red cabbage with applesauce. There are people around mommy. Certainly two women ... The midwife and a friend, yes that's it, her best friend ... And the four-year-old son who approaches quite timidly. The father is not there.

Below, on the ground floor of 10A Gasthausstrasse, the music has stopped, the last customer has closed the door carefully behind him; he has slipped off into the night, keeping close to the walls. He's cold. He doesn't wish to be seen coming from the brothel of the Jewish house. He looks like Herr Marcus Antonius, the official in charge of order and security. At the street corner a man in a gray shirt follows in lockstep behind. He has a black apothecary's skullcap clamped onto his head and his eyes are like two pin heads behind the thick lenses of his round glasses ...

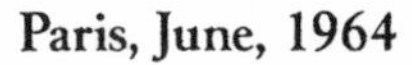

Paris, June, 1964

On the pavement in front of the Ambigu Theater's bookstore, night softens the light of streetlamps and the shop signs, the autograph-hunting cyclist has disappeared around the corner of Boulevard Sébastopol and the bookseller pokes his head around the glass partition's door to make sure that the unwelcome stranger has indeed gone away. *Tannhäuser* is turned down.

The owner of the place goes back to his counter and the celestial maps of St. Theresa. He lifts his arms, two wings of gray cotton–discouragement? resignation? "We'll figure it out yet," he promises me, he pushes his little glasses back on his nose and plunges back into his starry mysteries. "With Saturn in conjunction with the Sun, Theresa was able to show violence and stubbornness ... She suffers migraines which are the symptoms of her inner conflicts ..."

A light kiss has just landed on my neck. We used to call these caresses *papillons* (butterflies). Maxime places another on the lobe of my left ear to say "what a bore!" His hands hold mine and I feel the coin slipping that was to pay for the spangled portrait of that poor Theresa. How could we get rid of this old fellow carrying on with his visionary rigmarole?

"... Her search for the absolute leads her to a saturnine sternness, strips her of all guile ... With a Moon in Pisces, synonym for mysticism, transcendence is possible. This Moon in Pisces is the one of compassion, of charity, of self-abnegation, it reinforces her capacity for putting all her gifts at the group's service ... It's the sign of the union of hands ..." The bookseller lifts his eyes slightly, his gaze fixed on our clasped hands, sign of our union.

As I listened to the little man, I didn't know that I was happy, truly happy for the first time in my life–and perhaps the last as well; it's a pity—we ought to know about these things so we could make them last a bit longer or remember them better.

I didn't know that several months later I would find again my old friend, fear. The fear of being abandoned experienced by a small girl of three, that November morning when a thin, icy cold rain was falling. On the platform of a station in Germany, a woman in tears and a tall boy of seven let me board the train, they let me go, me under a large woollen cap, while they themselves went on to die without me.

"I'd very much like to cast your horoscope, mademoiselle. Would the gentleman mind?"

Mönchengladbach, August, 1989

Herr Marcus Antonius has come back to his chair beside the deputy mayor. My neighbors, the professor from Vancouver and the lady from Luxembourg bombard him with questions about security. Even the churches, even the cemeteries are no longer safe! What are you doing about this? Prevention or repression? "Repression—not that, the least possible ... You know we don't like that method any more ... It has cost us so much ... But it is very, very difficult; there are juvenile delinquents and then there are the real criminals, the latter are not just fooling around ... and the citizens have the right to feel protected, don't they?"

Marcus Antonius is quite annoyed and the deputy mayor looks a little bored.

The courier has come back; the envelope he hands Herr Marcus Antonius is much larger than the first. He thanks him with a wide smile showing his teeth which I am sure are all false. The interruption has changed the conversation. The American from Queens, New York City (a central point of the

Jewish diaspora shared with Afro-Americans) who claims to be close to the president of the United States, would like to have some details about the electoral system of West Germany. Herr Marcus Antonius breaks open the envelope. I stare at him. It's for me, that envelope, why is he opening it instead of me?

Paris, June, 1964

That evening I had forgotten my fear. It was buried, far off ... I was happy. The bookseller could say anything at all to me under his shiny, dirty smock, nothing would happen to me because Maxime was beside me. Since we had taken the plunge, made that foolish decision to unite legally, my fear of abandonment had disappeared.

For the first time I felt I could say this is mine: my room, my cat, my life. My husband. That word had been difficult to swallow, I had had to get used to it. I had fought it off for seven years, I didn't want anything to do with it, I didn't want it from Maxime or from anyone else. I only knew one thing that was mine, my freedom. But Maxime was persistent, patient and persistent. A chess player. I had told him about my childhood, the few things that I knew more or less from hearsay as well as the things I really remembered: the war, the occupation, the hiding, and all that.

He promised me that that would never happen again, never again as long as he was with me. Suddenly I so wanted to bury my fear, to make its grave there, in the middle of a concentration camp, or a nightmare, or whistling bombs, or on the platform of a train station in November, that I began to love him and to believe that it would be true. In that month of June, 1964 I was happy in the little bookstore of the Ambigu.

Maxime agrees to having my horoscope cast, he agrees to

everything; he's amused. The little glasses jump on the bridge of the proprietor's nose. "It takes awhile to calculate it—have you got the time?" "All the time in the world," replies Maxime "and look, while you consult your conjuring book I will bring in your postcard rack or else passers-by will think your shop is still open and you will be distracted all the time." Maxime takes things in hand; it's his nature. The bookseller finally notices him and is impressed by this young man who is so useful. "It's so rare," he says in a deploring voice. And taking advantage of the bargain, "You are so kind, young man, would you also pull down the iron shutter while you are about it?" I hear Maxime laugh. He loves the unexpected, and this evening that had begun with *Pierrot le Fou* promises to be even crazier than Godard's film. The bookseller has spread out a large map of the heavens, opened a notebook, and picked up a pencil that he begins to sharpen carefully. "Let's get down to business, mademoiselle, where were you born? City and *département*? Year of birth? Month? Day and time?" I hear the grinding of the iron grill come down and the beating of my heart picking up without reason, just like that. "I was born on a 25th of February ..."

Mönchengladbach, August 1989

"They should have given us one day off," complains Liesel, 82 years old and completely exhausted. "Enough is enough; we cannot keep up with it," adds Victor, 65 years old, grandson of a generous millionaire leather manufacturer who had once been called the most socialist of all the region's employers.

It's Sunday, we've been invited to a cruise on the Rhine. The boat is luxurious, lots of chrome, there is an overflowing buffet on a giant rectangular table, a still-life with the scent of herring, caviar, and thirty types of fresh bread. Little fat pigs made of pink marzipan, which complete the setting, cause some to grumble: "Pork! How insensitive!"

Outside on the river, the sky drips like a runny nose. No matter. No one is there to look at the scenery, people continue looking for others the way they have done from the first day. Loudspeaker announcements: "Mrs. Gerstein of Miami, maiden name Rothschild, asks all those who knew her family to make themselves known to her." "Mr. Pohl of Reading, near London, formerly of Odenkirchen, wants to meet Mr. Stein of Königstrasse, or any of the members of his family." "Does anyone have information about Mrs. Alexander, maiden name Leven, and of her little boy who were both deported to the ghetto of Riga?"... A curious sort of hide-and-seek has been going on for three days. People wandered about between tables in restaurants or aisles in churches and lecture rooms, from the first to the last rows in buses, in the hotels and museums. They stare at each other, trying to recognize a profile that was once young, cheeks which were once smooth, hair that was once red or brown, eyes that were not magnified by glasses ...

Several very old women have brought their daughters who are themselves old women. One of them always carries around her neck a photo taken of herself when she was nine. They look each other over, lie about their ages, whisper: "You noticed; it must be Julie Feldmann. How she is wrinkled! And that one over there, she has gotten fat, put on at least thirty pounds. I would never have recognized her." "Me—it's curious that everyone recognizes me right away," brags a ninety-year-old with a pallid look.

Tired of trying to spy each other out and solve riddles, the visitors have demanded name tags which they have pinned on their suits, their blouses, their dresses, their sweaters. "What luck!" the press officer confides to me, "they asked for it themselves. We had thought of it, obviously, even had the tags ready, but we'd never have dared to suggest it ourselves ... Just think: after the 'yellow star'!"

Watch out for blunders, faux pas; a misunderstanding happens so easily. The well-meaning reunion organizers are full of uneasiness. "Sometimes we ask ourselves whether too much tact doesn't risk being seen as offensive," the mayor confides to me while explaining why drinks are from a cash bar. A lady from Bogotá who had survived Birkenau laughs out loud, "You know, I feel sorry for them!"... A young American journalist who has come with his grandfather agrees, "Frankly, I would rather be in my shoes than theirs."

Paris, June, 1964.

"You are an astrologer?" asks Maxime after having brought in the postcard rack and lowered the iron shutter. He's exhilarated that evening, Maxime, he is ready for a good laugh, for he doesn't believe in destiny written in the stars, or seers or their visions, anymore than he believes in a God or His saints and apostles. Maxime is an agnostic, a real one, by birth, has always been one. For that matter I too do not believe in this God who played Pontius Pilate during the Holocaust, this strange God who let six million of his children go up in smoke. He does not appeal to me. If despite everything He did exist, somewhere, I would not want to speak to Him. Except once only, I would ask Him, "What did my mother do to You? What did my brother do to You? Why did You let them die like animals? Why did You let me live? Is it a punishment or a reward?" Clearly He would not tell me, my God of the Jews, He only speaks to rabbis and sages, not to me, someone who married a goy and does not believe in Him ... Or in astrology ...

The bookseller—that curious fellow—has kidnapped me as it were. In his eyes there is no sign of desire, that glint that comes into the eyes of men aroused by a good-looking girl. Yet his eyes fix on me and detain me in his shop. Maxime doesn't interest him at all; he ignores him.

"You are an astrologer?" Maxime repeats the question.

"Not really ..."

"You have studied it in a school?" Maxime persists.

"Not really ..."

If I interrupt will he become a little more talkative? "But then, how do you do it, with all your maps and calculations?"

"I have read up on it, mademoiselle, a great deal ..."

"You have learned it by yourself?" My question gets a smile out of him and jolts his glasses onto the ridge of his nose. He has gray teeth and a moustache with yellow hairs that I had not noticed before.

"During the War I was very much alone and I had time ... I was at La Trappe in Belgium ..."

"With the Trappist monks?" asked Maxime who has understood.

Me, I was thinking of a trap door, a hiding place: during the war hiding oneself was normal ... I had known many hiding places, I could see them passing by superimposed on the bookstore, the Ambigu Theater, and the Boulevard St. Martin: the apartment in Antwerp in the Jewish ghetto, my red scooter, uncle Max, my little coat of gray rabbit fur with its large buttons like sleeping kittens; then Brussels in that large street near the Place Liedts, there was a baker on the ground floor, and an enormous entrance gate; then Rue des Sicambres, the trains at the end of the dead-end street, strange meetings in the basement ... members of the Red Orchestra I found out later. Did I flirt with Leopold Trepper when I was five years old?

More hiding places, better disguised, a boarding school near

Bruges where they wanted to baptize me by force, where the good sisters never ceased saying that the wicked Jews had killed the kind little Jesus, and I cried and said, "It's not true." They sent me away, my head full of lice; the school had been bombed, by mistake ... Then a hospital or an old age home, I don't really remember anymore, it was in the countryside, a monk in farmer's clothes had taken me there in a farm cart. I saw cows in a field for the first time; I had never seen any before, not even in the picture book that my dear auntie-mommy let me leaf through, so I thought they were pigs, and I said it out loud to show my knowledge and they made a great deal of fun of the little Jewish city-girl in the cart drawn by a rickety mule.

I shared a room with a nurse who was very kind; she gave me a blue medallion that I have always kept, of the blessed Virgin, not to make me change religion but to protect me. "The Blessed Virgin loves all the children," said the nurse and I used to fall asleep reassured.

Then the village, Sorle-Saint Gery, something like that, the large farm, the white bread baked in the kitchen's oven, pancakes once a week, the milking of the cows, hot milk full of bubbles and flies, games in the attic with the mischievous little boys who pulled down my underpants to see if the private parts of a little Jewish girl were similar to those of their sisters and their girl cousins. They touched me a bit to be sure there was no real difference and I let them do it because they were the leaders and I was afraid and also because it gave me a strange sensation in my abdomen, a new sensation, sweet and strong, undoubtedly forbidden ... I will never tell anyone about it, ever. It was my first experience of sexual excitement and my last hiding place.

It was there, in the large basement of the farmhouse where all the village had taken shelter, that the Americans arrived to liberate us.

I hear Maxime's voice close to me. "That must have been a hard life for you in La Trappe?"

The bookseller rolls up the sleeves of his gray smock; "Hard? Not at all ... You must be joking. Those were the best years of my life, yes indeed."

Me, I am still in my hiding places, I burst out, "Still, Belgium was occupied, the Germans, the Gestapo, times were hard ..."

The bookseller sighs. "Ah, the Germans! If only they had won their war, *their just war.* Finally poor little Belgium would have been liberated along with France and the rest of the world, *freed from the Jews and other vermin.* And finally there would have been order. Those people, the Germans, mademoiselle, have a sense of order I assure you!"

Maxime is close to me. He doesn't say anything, but I understand: say nothing and let the man speak right to the end without contradicting him. My heart begins to beat in staccato jerks.

"The West lost its only chance of salvation, mademoiselle. If they had stayed, the Germans, they would have got rid of all that riffraff for us ..."

He points his finger at the meagre assortment of comic books where the little boy in the yarmulke had just been looking for *Flight 714 for Sidney.*

I am cold, I am hot; my hand reaches for Maxime's, it trembles. We say nothing.

Mönchengladbach, August, 1989

Herr Marcus Antonius thanks the courier who had brought him the envelope. He opens it absent-mindedly in the midst of replying to a question from the professor from Vancouver. He brings out an 8½ by 11 sheet of paper and glances at it. His voice changes slightly, his answer speeds up as if he wanted to get the professor's question over and done with as quickly as possible.

I try to catch his eye; I want him to give that certificate to me! His face has lost its color, the blotch on his nose has turned blue, his eyes no longer leave the document which he puts carefully on the table in front of him. I want to get up and snatch this bit of paper away from him which is no one's business but mine, but damn it, I am too well brought up to upset the meeting. A more lively discussion has just broken out between one of the visitors and one of the officials. I don't listen, I look at Marcus Antonius who has now turned quite red. He has brought out a handkerchief to wipe his brow, his right hand goes up and down like a piston between his brow and the table, his left hand squeezes the empty envelope. The envelope is crushed, his hand trembles.

I close my eyes to mere slits, I stare at his half-bald head and concentrate as strongly as possible. I become small again, very small, five years old, I press my nose against the window of a streetcar in Brussels, I hypnotize the soldier in the gray-green uniform who has lined up against a wall all the men who had been in the streetcar with us, my little mother and me. I am hypnotizing him because I don't want him to come and give us trouble; I am the one who can control him with my eyes fixed on the middle of his back, there, where his heart is beating. My little mother—I know that she's my aunt, the youngest sister of my mother, but when you are five years old you have to say mommy to someone—has such a sweaty hand that mine slips in its grasp as on wet soap. I was right to hypnotize that German soldier for he didn't even notice us, or else he pretended not to, but at all events he asked us nothing and we were able to go home on the yellow streetcar.

In the large conference room of the town hall of Mönchengladbach, Herr Marcus Antonius is unaware of my attempts at hypnosis, he doesn't even look at me when I order him to, no, on the contrary he appears to be avoiding me. He leans over to his neighbor, the deputy mayor, the one who fancies me a bit, he shows him the piece of paper which makes him blush, then grow cold, and his fingers tremble. The deputy mayor in turn goes red in the cheeks, he scratches his head, he's confused,... In me something tears open, a very, very old wound that I had thought healed, hurts again. I am afraid.

Paris, June 1964

"You said you were born on a February 25 ..." The Trappist-fascist bookseller takes up his calculations again. I am no longer afraid, for Maxime is there, nothing can happen to me; he promised me.

"In which *département*?" asks the bookseller. I am startled, he wakens me from a dream that is making me afraid. "In Mönchengladbach, I don't know the *département*, there aren't any, it's not here, it's in the Rhineland, in West Germany." The black apothecary's cap slips and reveals an almost hairless, ugly skull. "You didn't say you weren't from here. This complicates things." I regain my nerve, "You didn't ask me that, monsieur!"

Mönchengladbach, August 1989

In the streets there are no decorations or banners of welcome, but an elegant blue official poster covers a number of walls and official bulletin boards as well as decorating most of the store windows. Two rolls of the Torah set in the center of a Star of David are placed above this double title: "*They were and are our neighbors—*

Vestiges of Jewish life in Mönchengladbach." It is an invitation to remembering. Various testimonies inspired by the work of Günter Erckens, documents and archives have been assembled by the Christian-Jewish Society in the *Haus Zoar,* (The House of Zoar, place of refuge), the Protestant church's parish hall, a handsome building in post-modern style, red bricks, steel and large windows. The evidence of the Jewish presence in the region from the 13th century to the Shoah are exhibited there in two large rooms.

The exhibition is neat and well-organized. The city's archivist who organized it acts as guide to the visitors. She points out: "Discrimination wasn't an invention of the Third Reich. It had been common practice for a long time. Please don't take offence, but look at these two stained-glass windows from a Romanesque church from the Middle Ages ..." The archivist's head resembles that of a porcelain doll, the same glass eyes, the same rosy transparence of the cheeks, the same pale locks curled around the temples. She is very moved; she would like to communicate her knowledge as an objective historian, to vindicate through history what cannot be vindicated, but her audience today disturbs her and throws her off-balance.

"Indeed it was only after the occupation of the Rhineland by French troops in 1794, after the French Revolution, that Jews were treated as full citizens for the first time. Liberty, equality, you know what the French said at that time ... But alas that wasn't to last...." The archivist's voice spirals upwards and is lost under the high windows, the visitors that afternoon of August 1989 listen absentmindedly, as to a distant liturgical chant. This distant past—not really, thank you—doesn't interest them, they hurry on, and then stop thirty feet farther, adjust their glasses to catch the details of the yellowed photos hanging from picture moldings and read the captions out loud.

In this wing devoted to the 20th century, they are at home, they know more than the diaphanous archivist, it's their turn to tell her the small things of life that the history books never mention. "Look at him!" says Joseph from New York, "That's my uncle, how proud he is in his uniform. Wounded at Verdun, decorated four times. A national hero. That one there was Otto, his friend, a pacifist-anarchist who nonetheless went to war for love of Germany. Medals he wouldn't touch; I am not sure whether he refused them outright or just threw them into a drawer ..." "Ah, the main street!" exclaims a tiny ninety-year-old lady who has come from Florida, the state that is thought to be reserved for emigrant Jews in their retirements and final years. "The large store at the end, which forms the angle with the Marienplatz, it was there I did my apprenticeship in fine lingerie sales. At the time it was a promotion for a young girl from a good family. The owner was a distant cousin of my father's. And there, a few yards away, was the kosher butcher shop and the hairdresser over on the left. He was a Jew as well, a blonde Jew with gray eyes exactly the same color as yours, my dear Frau archivist."

The grandson of the industrialist Moses Stern, legendary patron of the arts after whom a street is called today, takes the guide by the arm. "I am going to tell you a Jewish story which they have been telling in London since 1940 and which is still funny...." The archivist listens with one ear and laughs politely, her other ear follows parts of the conversation of Mr. Bacher who is improvising a lesson for two students who have come to take notes in their exercise books. "Look!, there, that was my school in Rheydt. The last window of the second story, that was my classroom. Joseph Goebbels was in my grade, he was rather nice, very shy because of his clubfoot which made him limp and which got him off gym lessons ... Me, I got along well with him, he never referred to me as a dirty Jew, never. What, you don't know who Goebbels was? What do they teach you in your schools?" Mr. Bacher is short of breath. He puts the two students in front of the photo of his former school and expresses his indignation to his wife who doesn't come from here, who doesn't know ...

I too, I observe and I listen. I stop in front of a group of military men with large mustaches. "One of them is perhaps my grandfather," I say to the archivist. "At home I have a photo of him in dress uniform. He had the same mustache. He died in 1930. He didn't know Hitler. He didn't know me. He was a patriot." "Mustaches were very fashionable," chips in Mrs. Weyl who toddles along on the arm of her great grand-nephew. "In my street there were all sorts who wore them, they were often auburn, they trimmed them with fanatical care. These men were very attractive. Girls fell in love with them by the dozen. It didn't matter to them if they were Jews, my dear lady, that wasn't important. The girls didn't make distinctions. Besides, most of the men hardly practiced their Judaism; they only went to synagogue once a year, on Yom Kippur, the Day of Atonement. Once a year, that doesn't count, does it? They were peasants, blacksmiths, merchants, doctors, lawyers, industrialists, jazz musicians and popular novelists ... Good matches, very much sought after ..."

Mrs. Weyl keeps walking with short steps, her slight silhouette is lost in the middle of a group of six other visitors, still her voice dominates, sharp and shrill. But this voice is suddenly quiet, the others around her are equally silent.

We have arrived in front of the last set of pictures. Our guide the archivist is also silent, she stares at the photos taken in the camps by anonymous witnesses. She has no more comments to make. We had already seen photographs similar to the ones on display in newspapers, in books, or on television. These, though, have never been published—"Private Collections", says the catalog—but the emaciated bodies, eyes like holes, desolate barracks, having become dangerously familiar nightmares, remain unbearable ... I think I spot a face: "That one there, up high, in the middle, he could be my cousin...." Perhaps I will recognize my mother and my brother with his brown curls and moist eyes ...

There are cards framed in black, pinned up among the photographs: the list in alphabetical order of those who were deported and never returned. Oh, my God, thirty-six persons taken away and disappeared! That's on mother's side alone! There were that many? I hadn't realized that I was born into a large family. How I would like to be able to remember!...

A holiday, for example, only one ... Christmas, why not Christmas? I am certain that the Jewish children of Mönchengladbach celebrated Christmas with the other children, and I was three years old and I had wound garlands around a green plant in that large room above the brothel. Even the girls working on the ground floor had given me white and silver globes, gingerbread and little pigs in pink marzipan, and I had invited at least thirty cousins, boys and girls, to share the gingerbread with me, and all together we had sung "O Tannenbaum"... That was how things would be in a large family, surely ...

My mother's name is on one of the lists with the date of her birth and the date the convoy left that took her to the ghetto of Riga. It is the same thing for my brother. It does not tell when they died, it is only said that they left the city. There is a third name pinned to those two names, I read it and re-read it in sheer disbelief ... It's mine!... born February 25 ... deported on ... at age five. I have a bizarre sensation of being transparent, that somehow I do not exist. I start laughing. Little Mrs. Weyl stares at me in an offended way. I try to explain my discovery; "It's funny,..." but she looks so annoyed that I laugh harder and harder. I just can't stop myself.

The archivist approaches me. "You have a problem?" Whether I have a problem? She must be joking. "A very small problem, yes, one detail, look, it's me, it's my name, and I wonder—it really is uproariously funny isn't it—whether I am really me or whether I am someone else ..."

The archivist is mortified. The catastrophe that she feared so much has just come crashing down on her head. She had taken so much trouble to organize this exhibition, months and months of research, of reading, of correspondence exchanged with unknown people living in the four corners of the world, then wham! the one error that she must not at any price commit, to bury a living person with the murdered ... She has tears in her eyes, her unruffled demeanor is shaken, and she certainly is not used to crying, this lady archivist! I console her: "Come on, it's not serious; look at me, I am alive and well, that is the essential point. Mistakes are inevitable, after all. All you need to do is to make a little correction, you must have some correction fluid or an eraser ..." The archivist is about to throw up.

She explains that it isn't only on the cards on the wall, but it's also in the catalog, in the book of remembrance—over there on the lectern beside the seven-branched candelabra—and even in Volume II of Dr. Erckens' work where it says that the last place I lived was number 3, Goethestrasse. Goethestrasse! So, had my mother and brother at least been able to leave Gasthausstrasse, the street of whores, before they left forever? Where is it, this street of the daddy of *Faust* and of *The Sufferings of Young Werther*? Is it true that I also lived there, I,—born in a brothel and no less than four times declared dead by the age of five? I was lucky. Being alive became wildly comical in Mönchengladbach during that month of August 1989.

Paris, June 1964

A bare bulb sheds a meagre light on the bookshop counter. The dimness doesn't seem to worry the little man in the gray smock which is getting grayer all the time. He has found the city of Mönchengladbach on a page of his atlas, and now carries out detailed measure-ments with his compass and his ruler. "The time?"

I look at my watch: "Almost 10:45 p.m.; it's late."

Annoyed, he pushes back his little glasses. "At what time?" I don't understand, I don't reply.

Maxime comes to my help, "What exactly do you need to know?"

Thoroughly angry, his skullcap slips on his sweaty dome: "What time were you born?" I reply that I don't know. He's astounded. "You mean you don't know?"

I repeat that I don't know.

"You never asked your parents?"

"No."

"They never told you?"

"No," I repeat the word like a cracked record.

"You have a birth certificate? A card of identity? The time is not recorded on it?"

"No." I can't say anything more, my voice breaks inside me, I must remain calm and dignified, let this monster in a gray smock talk. A kind of nausea reaches my lips.

"You don't feel well, mademoiselle?" the bookseller asks in a concerned way. He drags himself out from behind his counter and gets me a shabby armchair. "Do sit down, mademoiselle ... This is going to take some time. Without your ascendant ... you understand?" I shake my head. "Our day of birth determines our sign: you were born under the sign of Pisces. But everyone also has an ascendant. Sometimes it can influence the sign strongly. To know this ascendant it's necessary to know the place and the time of one's birth. You are only giving me half the necessary information so this is going to be harder and take longer, mademoiselle. You will have to be patient."

I say nothing. I think I will not be able to say anything more this evening, my throat is so choked up. I huddle in a ball in the armchair and hold onto Maxime's hands. He looks at me continually. His blue eyes are on fire, he devours me with his love. I don't yet know that blue eyes can be like ice. The bookseller disappears behind his glass wall. It is Parsifal's "Good Friday Spell" by Wagner that floods over us. The music, like hypnosis, penetrates every pore of our skin. Parsifal, looking for what? I don't know the time of my birth, but I am sure that it was nighttime, winter, and outside a storm was destroying the world.

Mönchengladbach, August, 1989

With his plump hands the deputy mayor smooths the paper that Herr Doctor Marcus Antonius has just given him. He continues to answer his visitors' questions, but I get the impression he's only answering the ones which come from the end of the table furthest removed from me. Dr. Marcus Antonius pivots in his armchair and remains facing the same direction. I only see his back. Am I going to stand up, move the deputy mayor's hand from the white sheet, and nonchalantly carry the paper away?

What an idiot I am! I'm not moving! I stare straight ahead, I look at the table, the hands of the deputy mayor and the back of Herr Marcus Antonius. Finally he moves round toward the center of the table. His forehead glistens with drops of sweat. His left hand moves towards the sheet at the same moment that the deputy mayor puts his up to his mouth to cough. Marcus Antonius has taken back the fateful piece of paper. He tries to fold it lengthwise into thirds. He pretends to tear it up. His boss detects his charade and motions not to do it. I am still glued to my chair, unmoved and mute. What is happening to me? Usually I am the first to ask questions, to get discussions going, frankly to put my foot in it. I only have to ask aloud whether that paper is really meant for me! Or simply ask anything at all, however silly, so that they will be forced to turn in my direction. I don't move; I count the minutes which seem so long and the beats of my heart which seem so short ...

My neighbor from Australia who has said nothing up to now suddenly speaks up in a wispy voice that emerges incongruously from his massive body. He speaks directly to Herr Marcus Antonius and calls him by his first name, "Lieber Marcus Antonius,..." Marcus Antonius is trapped, he has to turn in my direction and I catch his eye with a fixed smile, my hands are making rings in the air "Here we go round the mulberry bush, the mulberry bush, the mulberry bush." I point to the paper and back to myself with the same finger. "That's for me, isn't it? How nice of you! Thank you so much ..." Herr Marcus Antonius gets up without having spoken to the large Australian; he walks over to me reluctantly, he holds the white paper away from himself, behind his head, as if he was trying to dry it ... I smell his breath on my neck. Herr Marcus Antonius must smoke large cigars.

"This document is an error, it may not be let out. It may not leave the walls of this town hall, it may not be photocopied ... That's the law ... They made a mistake down there on the ground floor in the registry office, they never should have ..."

He gets himself tangled up in his own explanations. "I can show it to you; if you wish, you can look at it!..." In the blink of an eye I reach out my right hand, grab the sheet, put it down in front of me and put both elbows onto it, my chin ensconced in the palms of my hands. "Don't worry, I will not make any professional use of this, Herr Dr. Marcus Antonius, but I am hanging onto it!" He knows he is not going to get it back. He has lost his gamble. But what was the gamble, exactly? What is at stake with this paper?

Paris, June, 1964

"It's strange, very strange ..." The June night has suddenly become thick and humid. A ceiling of inky black clouds hangs over the Ambigu Theater. The bookseller wipes away the streaks of perspiration which are running from under his skullcap. My astrological picture, my map of the heavens as he says, is giving him bouts of heat. "I don't understand ... What is missing ... What is missing ..." He mumbles his abracadabras; I catch the odd word: fourth-house, fire, planet, equinox, air, sun, water ... He takes up his compass and his ruler again, measures improbable distances, Mönchengladbach to Venus, draws circles that decide fates, perhaps ... I wonder if his maze goes as far as the camp where my mother disappeared along with the brother I would have wanted to be beside me ...

Maxime goes over to the counter to see what the old man is doing. He adopts a knowing attitude as if he had understood it all, as if he too were familiar with the mysteries of astrology. He has always liked to pretend ... "It's like a pit ... like a hole which had swallowed you since your earliest childhood. An eclipse ... a sacrificed home ... Father absent ... Mother ... I have never seen anything like it." The bookseller of the Ambigu is definitely puzzled. I knew from my grandmother who had survived Theresienstadt, that my father was a skirt-chaser and that my mother, a steadfast Penelope, had often wept. I was to think often of that mother, dead so young, gritting my teeth and vowing it wouldn't be like that with me.

"It's midnight." Maxime has just looked at the wristwatch I gave him for his birthday–his first birthday as a married man. The bookseller looks up.

I say "I'm thirsty!" I am happy, to hell with that antisemite and his black skullcap and gray smock ... "Let's go to the Place de la République and have a drink." The bookseller nods agreement, takes off his smock to reveal gray trousers and a gray shirt, removes the apothecary's skullcap, replaces it with a Basque beret on his gray hair. The last tones of Parsifal's "Good Friday Spell" still ring in our ears. Finally silence, a silence which lets you hear the dust falling off the high shelves from where Maxime had taken down the *Critique of Pure Reason.*

The clouds have opened up, it is raining large tepid drops that I let run down my nose. A June night's rain, like that of June 1943, Rue des Sicambres in Brussels, my nose pressed against the window, my eye fixed on the railway at the end of the cul-de-sac. I looked at the falling rain, jealous of its freshness, for I did not have permission to go out to let it fall on my bare arms.

Mönchengladbach, August 1989

"Hey, I know you! You are Alex Alexander's daughter!" the man who has just seized me by the arm is short and stout, with thin hair on an over-sized skull with a large forehead. His eyes sparkle with all the joy of a schoolboy meeting his best friend. "When I knew you, you were shitting in your diapers and him, he played poker. He was my buddy. We had a great time together. You have the same eyes, the same nose ... I noticed you right away." His name is

Joseph and comes from New York City.

"Alex, now there was somebody! A handsome fellow! Women were crazy about him, young or old they all fell in love with him." I had come here with the hope that someone would talk to me about my mother and my brother, that little boy with the brown curls and moist eyes. I didn't think, I am not sure why, that anyone would mention my father. Because he wasn't himself a native of this small place in the Rhineland? Or was it for a deeper reason within me that I wanted that man, that father, to remain in oblivion?

Joseph is happy. "You look like him, you are a good-looking girl. How old are you? Children? Husband?" Joseph wants to know everything about me; I am linked to moments of his life which he loves to remember. My being there, he tells me, makes his trip suddenly worthwhile. He had not wished to come, it was his older brother who had brought him. "He blackmailed me. He's old, he's sick, he needs a nanny, do I look like a nanny?" Joseph leans against the wall-bars in the gym; above his head is a basketball hoop with an overturned net.

We are in the multi-purpose reception hall of Mönchengladbach. The Christian-Jewish Society had rented it for a reception for the strange visitors in this month of August, 1989. Flowers, greenery and garlands, white paper napkins on long tables laid out with the buffet made up of "family specialties"—prepared by the committee's ladies—a stage, a choir, speeches, a string quartet, speeches, another choir, speeches ... "I hate them," says Joseph to me, "and all this fuss disgusts me. All these Jewish exiles who are thrilled to be here, who say thank you, thank you for the trip, the hotel and all the rest, these were the ones who early on felt the change in the wind. Ask them, you will see. They fled at the first signs of alarm between 1933 and 1935. They never saw personally how neighbors, friends, shopkeepers turned overnight into Jew-hunters. Me, I stayed until '39, so obviously my feelings aren't the same."

I'm on his knees, he bounces me. "There was a fine lady who had a white horse, giddy-up, giddy-up!" I scream with laughter, I wet my diaper.

"Oh! the messy brat, go see your daddy." He hands me over to Alex like a small parcel. I don't manage to make out his face, I only notice his skin, a very dull complexion ... It smells of beer around us, light beer and grilled sausage, there is a great deal of smoke, noise, and women heavily made-up come and kiss me, they resemble La Goulue and Marlene Dietrich in *The Blue Angel.*

I don't like their perfume of powder and sweat, I want my mommy who is upstairs in the apartment with flowered wallpaper and who is knitting sweaters for my dolls. This makes Alex Alexander laugh: "Sourpuss! you are better off with your daddy. You bring him luck! You have seen his four aces, haven't you? It's O.K., it's O.K., don't cry any more, you will go back to your mommy and never leave her again ..."

Would it be from that date that I have had this dreadful habit of suddenly crying? I would like to ask Joseph, but he wouldn't understand, he wouldn't know. I remind him of laughter and drinking bouts and a very sociable man who adored women and opera. "There wasn't a single aria from Italian opera that he didn't know. Three, four notes and immediately he recognized it, who was singing, who conducted the orchestra, and when ... Ah, to be a friend of his meant putting up with bel canto!" In New York Joseph had gone to the Metropolitan Opera several times, he had seen *Tosca, Il Trovatore,* and *Norma* "... along with two or three other things of the same nature," he says, all because of all those carefree moments stolen from the Nazis in the company of Alex Alexander and his little daughter who dirtied her pants ...

"I only came back once to the area, and it was intoxicating, believe me. April 1942, spring was making green splotches on the landscape over which I was flying in my bomber, 'made in USA.' I picked out the streets, the squares and I dropped the bombs and saw them destroy the haunts of my youth in bursts of fire and twisted metal and I exulted because I knew there would be a good collection of traitors and s.o.b.'s under the rubble. ..."

In the reception hall of the City of Mönchengladbach, Joseph told me all this. "That lot over there,"—he pointed out for me the crowd laughing and enjoying themselves—"they look like fine people, but I don't trust them, I cannot." He was among those who had escaped at the last moment, those who were able to get on the last boat going to Rio, a French ship called the *Chargeurs Réunis*.

"In March 1939, my girl; one had to be crazy to wait so long! Fortunately I got out just in time: after that all the exits were blocked."

My brother Gerd takes my hand; he is seven years old, he pulls me and it hurts, I have a bandage around my right thumb, I had cut myself in playing with mommy's sewing scissors. It is autumn. We are running together, the street is a dead end, it was necessary to take another, but it was the same, it is cut off by a patrol which is pointing large rifles at us. Over there is a garden with a privet hedge. "We will take a photo," Gerd says to me, "that way you will have a souvenir." Click! Click! Again the running. The platform of the train station.

Gerd stayed in the waiting room. He waves both his hands to say goodbye. My mother on the platform is wearing a pretty tweed coat with a collar of otter fur as soft as a rabbit. She is crying. Martha, the blond "Aryan" who will save my life at the risk of her own, says nothing, she lifts me up from the ground and puts a woollen cap on my head. After the war she will become my aunt, she will marry my uncle, my mother's brother,

Caroline Alexander and Gert, her brother, 1938.

a survivor of the camps where he had been sent thanks to a collaborationist police informer of the good city of Antwerp. "From now on don't say a word until we arrive, understand?" I nod with my cap to show I have understood. Martha kisses my mommy. Mommy kisses me and hugs me. Our tears mingle on our wet cheeks. The train leaves.

I am three years and seven months old. Eventually I will be a big girl and then I will grow old. My mommy on the platform is thirty-seven years old and will never have wrinkles, and Gerd in the waiting room will never have gray hair. In my hotel room in Mönchengladbach I have a photo that I will not show to Joseph: in front of a privet hedge, a little boy holds by the hand a very small girl in tears wearing a bandage around her right thumb.

Paris, June 1964

Maxime and the bookseller have lowered the shop's iron grill.

Why bother? Simply turning a key would have been enough. What is there that anyone would steal in this dusty lair? Several phonograph records from Bayreuth and the complete astrological profile of St. Theresa of Lisieux, her complete works as it were ... The sidewalk of the boulevard St. Martin is studded with stars, the reflection of the streetlamps on the wet pavement. The pub smells of rain, wet hair, cider and cigarettes.

We have some trouble finding a table for three, what we get is very narrow which upsets the Trappist-fascist bookseller; there is not enough space to spread out his chart and he has to fold his papers. Maxime and I order two glasses of white wine, the bookseller asks for a strong black coffee.

"We'll get there yet!" he tells me with a large smile as if to console me. If he only knew, poor idiot, what I had needed consolation for during so much of my life! "You were born Tuesday, the day of Mars ... The sun was in Pisces and the Moon in Aries ... The heavens have given you an open and pleasing personality. It is very clear, there...."

He shows me some signs in his illegible notation, using words I don't understand, which I don't even listen to "... Zenith in Libra ... Venus in Aquarius ... Mercury in Aquarius ... Intelligence, intuition, harmony ... Mysticism, yes ... and secrets, many secrets ..., a bubble ... Only something happened very early in your life which brought everything to a halt, complicated everything ... an event, a "sacrificed home," a sacrificed family, then between three and five years old, a total eclipse that plunged you into the night ... there is a void in your horoscope, mademoiselle, a void ... I don't see ..."

But I am beginning to see. Perhaps there is something true in this astrological alchemy, this game of stars and planets. I am afraid. Afraid of the unknown past, of the sound of boots, of synagogues in flames, of burned books, of smoke from the ovens of crematoriums, fear of being condemned to be abandoned, yesterday, today, tomorrow ... But Maxime is there, he is my rediscovered confidence, my refuge and my strength. Let this poor bookseller so nostalgic about the Nazis search out my eclipsed home, my void. Let him look for them in Wagner and the songs of glory of the Third Reich. He will not find them. For I am the one who knows where they are.

Mönchengladbach, August 1989

I have always been stumped by Gothic script. If it is printed I can manage after two or three lines. But handwriting, with its serpentine curves, its baroque consonants and juggled vowels! My copy of my birth certificate had been written by a deliberate hand, the hand of a schoolgirl who had learned to write out the Gothic curves without any breaks. It is clear, it is neat, I discover without too much difficulty the usual administrative terms, family name, first name, address of the parents and the child, its sex, date, time and place of birth.... February 25, girl, Gasthausstrasse, 3 a.m., *alles in Ordnung* (all is in proper order) ... At the bottom of the page is Alex Alexander's signature, I recognize the writing, I had read some of his letters and, even once, at the beginning of the war no doubt, I had received a postcard.

Herr Marcus Antonius puts his long hand on the document's right margin. "Don't be put off ..." I push away his hand. "You will laugh, but it happened to me too during the same period ..." This time hasty administrative writing, in a zigzag across the margin's narrow space, is scarcely readable. "It was the law, the legislation had just been passed, no one was able to avoid it,..." babbles Herr Dr. Marcus Antonius. What is he talking about? What is the importance of these scrawls that are like hieroglyphics to me? I decipher one word: "Sara" and a number "1938." "Just think, my parents had named me David–that shows they were not antisemitic," continues Marcus Antonius wiping his brow. "Well, believe it or not, but those idiots came to our house and demanded that my name be changed. Jewish first names were forbidden to Aryans." *Rassenschande!* (racial disgrace)–even in the vocabulary! "So my parents, to make sure there would be no more confusion, rechristened me in Latin ... Marcus Antonius! You can see–the notes in the margin of the record of birth–that could have happened to anyone!"

Fritz, Wilhelm, Otto, Rolf, Manfred, Heinrich, Karl and many other good little Germans with blue eyes were summoned by their town hall from August 18, 1938 on, in order that "Israel" could be added to their everyday names. For women and girls, the choice came from the name of Abraham's wife who bore Isaac at the age of ninety years: "Sara." On papers of identity, on the records of the state, Irmgard, Marlene, Christel, Martha, Gertrud, Ingeborg, Karoline were enriched with a second first name, symbol of longevity and fertility.

I was two years old and I don't know whether it was Alex Alexander or my mother who brought me into the Gestapo's offices. Probably neither of them, the presence of small children wasn't necessary. I had stayed in the garden surrounded by privets, Gerd was teaching me to play hopscotch. I kept stumbling on my little legs, the black gravel stuck to my left knee, I sobbed, Gerd would laugh heartily and hug me against himself. It had not been long since he had taught me to walk.

"I had a terrible childhood with that blasted Latin name," Herr Dr. Marcus Antonius whispers to me, "Everyone made fun of me ... You have no idea of the trauma produced for an adolescent by a little thing like that!" I read and re-read the text amended in haste in the margin that had suddenly become more important than the page. Lower down a different hand had added: "The above law is null and void from this day on, 23rd October, 1949." I look at Herr Dr. Marcus Antonius, he did not have the advantage of this annulment. I smile at him. "Poor Marcus Antonius, how I pity you"!

Paris, June 1964

The wine that a tired waiter serves us is a Gewürztraminer, one of those wines that pleased the palates of the apprentice gourmets that we were. We liked the glasses used for Alsatian wine, round balloons anchored to long green stems, and we had promised ourselves to get a set of six to celebrate our coming anniversary. The bookseller had kept his Basque beret on his bald head, only a few gray curls strayed out onto his neck. His coffee was getting cold, his face formerly as gray as the hairs of his beard, became animated. "You are travelling a route that is very dear to you, but you will leave it before next March. I see you taking a parallel direction, close to the one where you are now. You will be brilliant in it some day..."

I have had enough of the little glasses sliding down his sweaty nose, this twisted smile, this look which melted over me, which was trying to swallow me ... A bitter taste of bile mixed in my mouth with the Gewürztraminer's freshness, I still feel nauseated. "I am tired, I would like to go home." Maxime pays the bill.

The bookseller appears to be disappointed. "Already? I have not finished ... It takes a long time because of the time of birth that mademoiselle doesn't know. There is a void, and that other thing that seems to have disappeared from the heavens ... I would be able however to tell you a few things anyway. About your future. As for the past ..., the past escapes me. But for tomorrow, I can see, I can see ..." "Don't trouble yourself," says Maxime, "it's late." "It's late," repeats the bookseller and he folds up his charts carefully taking meticulous care not to spill any wine or coffee on them.

Suddenly I am sorry for him. I see myself, skinny and pale, under the hot summer sun of 1945. We were at the seaside, at

Blankenberghe, a popular beach resort in Belgium. Our first vacation. The first aroma of fresh bread in the bakery next door to the little rented apartment. I used to get up, sometimes at six in the morning and rush down the stairs barefoot, run over the cobblestones chilled by the night and stop in front of the basement where the bread oven was in its glory. It was magic, and magic were those shops where they sold real chocolate and strange fruits—oranges, bananas ... The butcher shops intimidated me, I had never imagined so much meat, entire quarters of steers with their tails dangling, and I asked myself who would be able to eat all that.

On the promenade a convoy of prisoners advanced at a slow pace in order to allow the population to insult the defeated, children to throw stones at them, others to spit on them.

They were young men, their uniforms were in tatters, they marched bent over, their hands over their shaved heads. They had brought me to see the spectacle, we didn't want to miss it, we wanted to scream out our scorn and our hate. I remember the emotion that I suddenly felt in my heart. I was discovering compassion ... The same sad compassion inspired in me by that Trappist-fascist bookseller of the Ambigu, twenty years later, a June night in 1964.

Mönchengladbach, August 1989

Tom, his hair tied in a ponytail, his jeans hanging loosely over the top of his sneakers, looks at age forty like the benevolent ghost of a hippie. Tom is not Jewish. He nurses his adoptive father, Professor Hoffmann, philosopher, professor of German literature and history at San Jose State College in California. The professor, aged, a blue beret clapped onto his bald head, looks like a grandpa who had escaped from a Basque fairy tale. I could see him trotting along in a comic strip, a loaf of bread under the arm and a Camembert in his picnic basket. German, and much more German than Jewish for nearly fifty years, hero of the trenches of Verdun, on the *other* side of the future Siegfried Line ...

In a few days after the meeting at Mönchengladbach will have ended, the German Federal Republic's authorities will organize a ceremony for him. Professor Hoffmann, the philosopher-patriot, will be solemnly decorated and entertained by the children and the grandchildren of the those who formerly drove him out.

Tom is a poet. He doesn't take offence at this masquerade, he laughs at it, but especially he takes care of the old man, he cuts his meat in his plate for him, he makes him take his medicine, he takes him back to the hotel when the evenings stretch out too long in nostalgia and cigarette smoke. Then he comes back and sits down quietly among the ladies with white hair and the gentlemen with the shining pates. He's here, he's there, he takes notes in a spiral notebook. "I have to remember for him, you see," he confides to me, "He forgets recent events almost immediately. But as for the past, the distant past, he's a living encyclopedia!"

Tom likes to talk with me, and I, I like to hear him, perhaps because we look like two urchins among these ancients. In the '60s he had studied engineering without really knowing why. He dragged his rebellion against the war in Vietnam along with him through university campuses. Professor Hoffmann was looking for a student to copy out a manuscript that he had just written on the life of Einstein. This was Tom. "I went home to the commune where I lived, and I told my friends that I had just met someone who would change my life."

Tom learned German, studied Einstein and collaborated on a second volume. Two years later, Professor Hoffmann, whose entire family had been exterminated, adopted Tom according to

American law. Father and son were at Mönchengladbach, two intersecting fates among so many others gathered together here for a strange pilgrimage.

Such was the case of Rabbi Harf from Buenos Aires, who passed his examinations for the rabbinate in Berlin in March of 1939: "The degree was practically given to us! There was no one left to supervise us. The questions had been sent, God knows how, from the Grand Rabbi in Jerusalem, there were two of us writing the examination in a library, and all the books with the answers to the questions were within arm's reach ..."

Rabbi Harf laughs with good humor. He laughs often, and when he does, meteors of tenderness flash in his eyes. He laughs with Ruth his forty-year-old daughter, a lithe and gracious woman who speaks German with the accent of the tango. I liked her immediately and the feeling was mutual; we spent a lot of time together with her rabbi father and with Tom after he had put to bed his heroic dad, remembering without commemoration, having fun without frenzy, holding hands simply for the sweet sensation of skin touching skin ...

When Rabbi Harf spoke in public, something which inevitably happened to him frequently, even here in Mönchengladbach, his voice dropped by two pitches, swelled with power, and his words, always wise even when passionate, were hard-hitting and sonorous.

"We have come. Our reason told us: 'Don't go,' our hearts whispered 'go.' Those who are here have listened to their hearts. They were right, for with their luggage they have brought their memories, the memories without which the reconciliation so greatly wanted by our hosts would be impossible. Let us forgive, but not forget. Let us know how to remember and say together as we say in Argentina, *Nunca mas!*, Never again!"

Ruth echoes: "*Nunca mas!* "I add: "*No pasaran*" (they shall not break through) as if to myself alone.

We are the last ones in a deserted bar, Ruth, Tom, Rabbi Harf and I. We take several photos with our arms around each other, we make our Schnapps last. The waitress begins to pile up the chairs on the table; she says nothing, she doesn't dare. With the same clientele, but in another era, she would have barked *Raus!* (get out!)... It really is late, we go our ways, and night falls on our shoulders like an eiderdown.

Paris, June 1964

We never knew the name of the bookseller of the Ambigu. He never introduced himself and we never asked him his name. Later on I could have asked my friend Christian Casadesus, the unhappy manager of that beautiful theater. It soon sank under the waves of the rising tide of commercial development, while above its ruins hovered the ghosts of heroes from tragedies and comedies who had laughed, danced, and cried in its gold, velvet, and crystal chandeliers... But the name of that little man had no importance. Besides he never bothered to ask us our names, he, the seer, the blind magus who thought he could read the stars, who called me mademoiselle and treated Maxime as if he were a nobody.

The rain has ceased, the June heat has almost dried the pavement, several patches here and there shine like cats' eyes in the night. The Place de la République has resumed its animation, the idlers have come out from the bistros where they had taken shelter. We remain motionless in front of the Grande Café du Cadran; the bookseller at our sides makes no sign of moving.

"Well, good night monsieur," says Maxime in clearing his throat.

"You are going far?" asks the bookseller.

"Boulevard Beaumarchais."

He says he will go with us for a bit, he still has two or three things to tell me. He looks unhappy, alone in the world, and we seem to be, in that night of June 1964, the only thing he has to hang onto. "The last métro leaves in twenty minutes, I have time to accompany you to Les Filles du Calvaire."

Boulevard du Temple, Boulevard des Filles du Calvaire, Boulevard Beaumarchais, three names with no connection and no logic for one single long avenue linking together those symbols of France, la République and the Bastille. We lived upstairs from the courtyard, in about five hundred square feet, whose windows looked out on a sea of gray roofs touched with pink. It was my first home, I was proud of it, and I loved its sweetness fixed up with mere pennies. I had bought it not expensively—the neighborhood wasn't fashionable—with that little nest-egg from reparations for my war losses, absurdly called "compensation for loss of schooling."

The bookseller who had promised more predictions says nothing. He walks silently beside us, his eyes half-closed behind the thick glass lenses. We too have no desire to talk. *Pierrot le Fou*, St. Theresa, the little boy in his yarmulke, the cyclist who collected autographs, Parsifal's "The Good Friday Spell" and *Tristan's* "Liebestod" (Love Death), the Third Reich's song of glory, my eclipsed home, that celestial enigma which had been mysteriously swallowed up—all that dances in my head and I have only one desire, to fall asleep in our large white bed. What more had this old fool to tell me, this pitiable hermit who had not understood anything at all and who thinks he holds the key to hidden knowledge? We stop at the corner of Rue Froissart. He holds out his hand to me, I keep mine in Maxime's.

Mönchengladbach, August 1989

I have folded the page where the Gothic letters seem to jump all over the place; with great care I have slipped it into a zippered money-pouch, and put it neatly at the bottom of my carry-all purse. The meeting with the town councillors finishes. The coffee in its flowered china cups is cold, dry biscuit crumbs lie on the tablecloth and the plush carpet.

A mini-bus waits for the guests to take them to their respective hotels. The deputy mayor says to me: "I'm taking you back. Just one telephone call to make. Wait for me in my office."

Gasthausstrasse, 3 a.m., Sara ... I have learned all sorts of things this morning. What if I had been able to give those clues to the Ambigu's bookseller ... that funny little man in the gray smock who was enamored with astrology and had cultivated an irrational hatred of Jews?... What would he have told me? That the man who held my hands and whom I adored was not exactly the ideal hero of my dreams? And today, now that I know, would life have been different or easier? Thanks to the "Archer," this horse with a human torso who aims at infinity, my ascendant Sagittarius, my amateur-astrologer girl friends will finally be able to explain my sorrows and my laughter. Water and fire ... Will the water put out the fire? Will the fire evaporate the water? There must be struggle within, within me.

I know some of them will laugh and say it figures that I was born in a brothel. They will make fun of me gently, they will say: "There is no such thing as chance."

Never again will a rabbi dare to ask if I am really Jewish, like the idiot at the Maimonides School where I had just registered my son. "Your family name could be Jewish or not ... It goes both ways. And your first names are not Jewish at all. Tradition says that you should always add a Biblical first name to a child's name!"

Where did this man come from? The Planet of the Apes? What good were his darling yeshiva and his precious studies, if he didn't know why in 1936 Jews in Germany had good reason to avoid distinctly Jewish names?

Tradition ... How fortunate for it that there was a Hitler to restore it on the official documents!

"So, you have got what you wanted?" The deputy mayor is all smiles. "You are very beautiful." His after-shave smells of clean linen. He is next to me, very close. He touches my shoulder lightly, his hand makes its way down toward my back. Is there an attraction between the executioner and the victim? He is not my executioner, I am not his victim, but our lives, our stories in history make this moment in this opulent office, with the blood in our veins pulsing faster, perverse.

"How lucky you are to work in such a nice office. The view onto the garden is so restful." I have slipped over to the window. He has not moved.

"It's an ancient abbey. It wasn't bombed. A miracle."

"I know, it's the abbey whose monks gave the city its name. You explained it to me."

In the courtyard the official Mercedes with its chauffeur waits for us. There are road repairs on Gasthausstrasse, it's blocked off. "Sorry, we are going to have to go a few yards on foot." The deputy mayor has almost recovered his composure.

I joke with him, "In any case, we'd have done better had we walked from the start; the town hall is five hundred yards away and we've been driving in circles for a quarter of an hour."

"... Protocol, my dear, protocol...." He takes me by the arm. Again this warmth, just a hint ...

"I had thought it would be much uglier...." In front of us is 10A joined to the side of number 10. Around the duplex, vacant land ...

"After the bombing everything was destroyed in the area, they tore down the ruins, rebuilt, except for these two houses which have a charming 1920s style. They should have been torn down ..." Everything was destroyed ... When? The fieldstone's gray is turning a sooty black. There are curtains in the windows, those of the ground floor are in tatters behind three pale green plants. The three second-floor windows seem less abandoned, with their triangular cornices over their recesses.

"It's so typical of the style," the deputy mayor comments, "That's the reason why the house wasn't demolished. You have noticed what happened to the rest of the neighborhood."

Above the doorway, the washed-out traces of a sign: *Pelzwaren*—(furs)... A furrier as the front man for a brothel? My father was a merchant, Joseph had told me. In the fur trade? No, here he was only a tenant they put up with ...

"If you wish, I will take your photo in front of the house!"

I hand over my camera to the Herr Doctor. I pose shivering in the door's entrance. The wind lifts my white linen skirt.

The wind had already blown here, and I had already worn on the step of this door a white linen skirt with flounces of starched lace. Mommy had photographed me here and one of the tenants had come out laughing and kissed me, leaving red smears of lipstick on my cheeks. Gerd liked very much that lady who gave him a perfumed handkerchief and who gave us marzipan in the shape of pink pigs. Then the lady had photographed us three:—mommy, Gerd, and myself on the brothel's porch. And my father who had just won at poker inside, came out, merry, a little drunk, followed by Joseph and he invited us all to celebrate at a restaurant, in one of those rare nice restaurants where Jews were still admitted. The maître d' lifted me up, "What a treasure, this little blackbird, a real doll!" He held me close.

"Poor angel ..., sad ..." He had the gentle look, a little sad, of the deputy mayor.

Paris, June 1964

At the corner of Rue Froissart and the Boulevard des Filles de Calvaire it's past midnight when I realize that the little gray man in front of me, who is holding out a hand I do not want to shake, has awoken in me old memories that I had thought were buried forever, sleeping the eternal sleep of forgetfulness in the love and the confidence of Maxime.

Again I realize that I will never know anything about where I first lived. For a long time there has been no one left to tell me about it, to make me laugh at my first mistakes, or to tease me about my first tears. I will never know the hour of my birth—it wasn't shown on the identity card required for my marriage to Maxime—no one would ever calculate the sign of my ascendant and astrology fans like the antisemitic bookseller of the Ambigu Theater will have to be left without answers.

He is a pathetic figure, really, he's not able to leave us despite his first attempt at a goodbye. "I would like to wish you good fortune, mademoiselle, but it's not in my power ... Your horoscope is informative despite that ... despite that "void," I mean the "eclips,e, the "sacrificed home" that ... You have felt cold, very cold, but today there is warmth in you. You have to protect yourself to keep it. You will often be worried, for your life will be one of passion and love. You are born for many conquests yet only for the love of one man, the man with whom you will grow old. You must some day find the man who will replace for you the eclipsed home, and who will finally make you happy ..."

He doesn't look at Maxime. "Good-bye mademoiselle." He turns his back on us, changes his mind and once again offers me his hand. I refuse to hold out mine, I cannot touch him; I can't help it. A superstitious fear—perhaps that hand is contagious. Perhaps he will contaminate me with a new antisemitism? I say: "The 'sacrificed home' was my mother. You got it right, monsieur. She died at Auschwitz." A lie. She died at Riga in Latvia. But the tragedy of all those places resound in that name "Auschwitz."

Mönchengladbach, August 1989

Classroom A. of the school (Gemeinschafts-Hauptschule) of Odenkirchen, formerly a village, now a suburb, is buzzing this morning. The twenty-seven students and their teacher have been on the job since 7 a.m.

They had lit the bread-ovens the day before, they have kneaded the raised dough, have taken the cakes and the pies out of their pans, whipped the cream, squeezed orange juice, prepared teapots and coffee makers, glasses, flowery plates, forget-me-nots and mimosa, cutlery in Solingen stainless steel ...

On the first floor, in the building's largest classroom, the children have prepared a huge U-shaped table. The overlapping tablecloths are real white cotton damask, but the napkins are paper. Tania, Zahide, Anke, Stefanie, Karl, Rolf, Eva-Maria, those who fuss feverishly around the teacher are between thirteen and fifteen years old. For six months the teacher has directed and encouraged their researches on the Hitler years, she has made them read *The Diary of Anne Frank* and other books which they have discussed together in class. They have seen films and photos, cut articles out of newspapers, written their commentaries with thick felt-tipped pens on sheets of kraft paper, drawn pictures, asked questions still unanswered, and they have put up on the classroom's walls the complete results of this exploration of the dark caverns of Hell, a display to be shared with us. This last Wednesday of August, everything must be ready before 10 a.m., for at 10:15 the class will receive visitors from another world.

There will be Manfred, my cousin, survivor of Theresienstadt, Auschwitz, Birkenau, and Buchenwald, deported at the age of eight. His wife Christa only knows about his suffering through scraps of conversation and screams during his nightmares let out nightly for the past forty years.

I also will be there, I who have nothing to tell and everything to learn. And also present will be my little mother, mommy's youngest sister. She, who so carefree, believed she would be looking after her niece only for a few weeks of transition without suspecting that those weeks would last a lifetime, and that she would now be looked after by her niece, a fair return of tenderness.

My little mother is the queen of the reception. This school used to be her school. The building, brand-new and all modern, is not the same, but it was built on the old site and has the same name "*Hauptschule an der Kirschhecke*". The principal of the school, along with the music teacher, the pastor of the Protestant parish, and two other teachers, have this morning dressed with special care to cope with "the" occasion.

They have stage fright. So do we. The children greet us with a welcoming song in Hebrew. The principal has a lapse of memory that reduces four students, three little Gypsies and a blond curly-haired Turkish boy, to helpless laughter. The teacher is so moved that she loses the thread of her speech.

We look at the panels of the display: "The children of the Star of David have touched our hearts. Slogans and phrases that pained us: 'Entry forbidden to Jews and dogs.' 'Jews out!' 'Jewish store, do not enter!' 'Swimming pool reserved for Aryans only.' 'Jewish children must wait outside.' "

Tania, one of the students, is my guide, her round, chubby cheeks are flushed under her short auburn hair. She tells me about the panel she has done with Eric, her friend the Turk, based on Hilde Sherman's *Zwischen Tag und Dunkel* (Between Day and Darkness) and Johanna Reiss' *Und im Fenster, der Himmel* (Through the Window the Sky), two books which the teacher had recommended to them but that had not been on the required reading list as was *The Diary of Anne Frank.* Tania had read them at home, but not many others had done the same; some were not interested at all and preferred soccer; others were indifferent, but all without exception had taken part in the preparation for that morning, "a great day"! Tania had chosen my place to be on her right, at the large U-shaped table.

"You have *really* seen the Eiffel Tower? And you went up it? Often? Paris is really large? As large as Mönchengladbach? Like Cologne or Düsseldorf? I was in Cologne once; it's huge, then Paris is even larger ..."

I tell her that size is of no importance, there are certainly many cities larger than Paris, but ... "Paris is the most beautiful of all." Tania envies my love of my Paris. "It must be a funny feeling to walk about the streets that you love the way you love a person." I promise to show her all these treasures if she comes to see me some day. She writes my address down in her notebook with her elbow placed so her neighbor can't copy it. While we chat like old friends, eating slices of warm bread and pieces of cheesecake, we have stopped following the speeches.

Suddenly we hear the voice of Manfred, my cousin who as a child was herded to Auschwitz. The buzz of individual conversations in the schoolroom dies away totally. "The tenth of November 1938, I had gone to school like any other morning and I saw the synagogue which had just finished burning. I had slept deeply and heard nothing. There was a large crowd gesticulating and yelling, children from my class throwing stones at the already broken windows. I saw some who were crying, some who were laughing, and some who were denouncing the Jews and saying that they were only getting what they deserved.

"The policeman, Karl, came up to me, I knew him well. He asked me, 'Where is your father?' I told him that I didn't know; daddy didn't get on well with mommy, so he had gone away some time ago, some said to Belgium, but I didn't know. The policeman said 'Show me your hands.' I showed them to him as I did at home to show they were clean and Karl, the policeman who used to come from time to time to have coffee with my grandmother, put handcuffs on me. He shouted, 'To the clink with you, dirty little Jew! In prison you will probably remember where your father is.' "

There is dead silence in the classroom, no one moves, even the noise of eating has died away. "That was the way it all began," says Manfred, "I was eight years old."

Irma, the teacher, tries to catch my eye. Will she dare ask a question? To ask this large man of fifty-nine, sweet as a teddy bear, speaking like a child, to tell what followed? It is the pastor who dares in a timid, hesitant voice, "Would you perhaps tell the children one or two things which happened to you in the camps?"

Manfred laughs, a good, big laugh, and points at me. "It's because of her; I didn't want to come myself, I have been asked a hundred times already, I have always said no, but once she was here, my cousin, and also along with my aunt, and with everything that the city has done these past days to make sure no one forgets, I let myself be convinced and here I am."

He takes a handkerchief out of his pocket, wipes his brow, takes the thermos on the table in front of him and pours another cup of coffee.

"We never talk about it, those of us who came back; it's not worth it, there are some who would not even believe us, it was so unbelievable, you can't explain. Nobody can explain it. I have never talked about it, not even to my wife, nor to my cousin there, but, since I have come, I am going to tell you ..."

And Manfred starts telling. His hoarse voice gradually becomes clearer, he speaks very naturally, as one would speak of a business problem about taxes, or about a contract, or about a film. As I listen to him I watch the adolescents' faces around me and that of the teacher which is covered with tears and that of the pastor which remains impenetrable, and that of the director who twists his hands nervously and that of my little mother who is very upset because she has spilled something onto her pretty blouse. Manfred tells how he was moved from prison to prison and from city to city: how at Frankfurt, two years after being arrested, he found himself amidst a large number of children. "There were a thousand of us when the war broke out. They took us out of the prisons and dispersed us among the camps. I am the only one who came back."

Manfred tells of Theresienstadt where he found *Oma*, his grandmother, my grandmother (our grandmother!) who did the housekeeping for a senior officer. Manfred makes us laugh, he played tricks on the officer and the other SS men. He was cunning, he knew how to get at the garbage first to steal the potato peelings and anything else that was edible for his *Oma*, the grandmother who had become so thin from hunger. The officer, fond of resourceful little Manfred, looked the other way; he was fond of the *Oma* who was discreet, well-educated and a good housekeeper.

"One day I did not find her in the usual place where I used to give her what I had managed to snitch during the night. I looked for her everywhere, I was beside myself, I knew she was ill and that the ill ... Well, a *kapo* a prisoner made guard finally told me she had been designated for a convoy of other sick people to be sent to Auschwitz for treatment.

"I knew, I no longer know how or from whom, but I knew what 'treatment at Auschwitz' meant. I ran everywhere until I found the officer in his apartment that no one had cleaned that morning, I fell at his feet, I cried, I raised such a hell of a row that the officer went out and got *Oma* out of the convoy on the pretext she was indispensable for his kitchen or some other thing.

"I had known how my grandmother was eventually taken to Switzerland by the international Red Cross that had come to inspect Theresienstadt. What I didn't know was that it was part of a trick: In exchange for the old and the very ill, the Swiss had promised some prisoners of war. They kept their word, they sent them back to Germany. When the prisoners got there, they were shot as they got off the train. To the SS they were nothing but deserters ..."

Around me the faces become more and more taut. The teacher has become a statue. Tania, beside me, doodles without looking ... "How did you manage to survive?" the pastor asks Manfred, again after coughing.

"I stayed a long time to take care of my grandmother. I was the one they sent to Auschwitz, then Birkenau, then Buchenwald ... I made myself useful, I did anything at all to show I was able. They were testing me, they made me carry the bodies out of the gas chambers, I had to put them into carts to push them to the ovens ... I knew that if I were to say no or if I looked weak, I would join the dead, I knew. Nights there were sometimes people who could not take it any longer and who threw themselves on the barbed wire to make an end of it. They were electrocuted; they stuck to the wire and I was the one who had to pull off the bits of flesh ...

"I was twelve years old, it was a long time ago ... When the Americans liberated us at Buchenwald, some of us died because they were given too much to eat. Me, I recovered, I was strong.

"They sent me to Paris with a group of survivors and I slipped away to see the Eiffel Tower. This is the funny part: the French police arrested me because I was German. It was all the same to me, what I wanted was to see the Eiffel Tower, that was my personal victory."

Tania on my left is white as a sheet. The teacher hides her face in her handkerchief, the three little Gypsies cry quietly. There are no more questions, nothing more to say. Manfred has spoken for the first time in forty years ... "So," he adds with a slight shrug of his shoulders, "now you know a bit about it, don't forget it, but I think we should change the subject."

He is giving the signal to relax, he lifts up his massive frame and asks the children to show him their projects. Tania sticks close to me. "*He too,... the Eiffel Tower ...*"

Paris, September 1989

I have often relived that hot June month and the bizarre evening spent in the Ambigu's bookstore. Maxime and I have told it to several close friends, and our friends were most impressed. Still today I remember it as if it were yesterday. I still see, on the corner of the Rue Froissart and the Boulevard des Filles de Calvaire, that little gray bookseller suddenly shrinking under my reply and I hear the word "Auschwitz" echoing on the walls of the houses, losing itself under the balconies, running along the narrow streets towards the Rue de Turenne, the Rue de Bretagne, the Rue des Rosiers, the *shtetl*, the Jewish quarter of Paris.

That poor old idiot who believed in hateful values and who had the misfortune to take an interest in a young Jewish customer who had come in to buy a postcard of St. Theresa of Lisieux with a halo of gold spangles. I don't know whether he blushed or went pale, he made three steps backwards, suddenly turned, sped up, a gray streak running in the dark toward the métro. The métro swallowed him up. We never saw him again, the Ambigu Theater was demolished, a fit ending to the famous "Boulevard of Crime."

Mönchengladbach, August 1989

They all came to say goodbye to us in the hotel lobby. The mayor and his deputy, Dr. Marcus Antonius, the press officer, and the archivist, that unlucky organizer of the exhibit. We hug, wish each other well, we thank each other, on one side for having come from such a long way, on the other for having been so welcoming.

There is a great deal of emotion in the air, American ladies with blue hair say goodbye to bald Argentinean men and bearded Australians, they exchange addresses which they will lose and make promises they will not keep. They say "we will come back" and know they never will. I brandish the large white paper with its secret and say "Thank you so much" to Herr Marcus Antonius who pretends not to notice my gesture. The deputy mayor would like to get closer to me, but the crowd is too thick and he's grabbed by two small chattering old ladies.

In the hotel lobby suitcases are piling up amidst announcements: "The limo for Cologne airport will leave in ten minutes!..."

... Everything is deserted, no one is left. The cold wind numbs my cheeks, I cling to my mother's coat, nestling against her long legs, a whiff of warm air very sweet and perfumed falls on my forehead. "Don't worry, everything will be all right," says young Martha. I put my head against mommy's right thigh, her muscles twitch slightly and I know she is crying and I, I try not to. I hear her faintly, "Yes, yes I will join you as soon as ...," the end of her sentence dies away, my vision also dies away along the platform, far, far; I am lifted up, someone puts a large woollen cap on my head, I let myself be carried like a little sack, in the compartment I cling to my future Aunt Martha, I hide myself, I don't see mommy getting smaller on the platform, nor Gerd who writes large letters in the air. The train has left, I don't move. My aunt's sweater is wet and tastes of salt. I am three and a half years old and my body empties itself of all its tears....

The schoolteacher and Tania hug me, they cry. "You will come back to see us?"

Tania, suddenly approaches me in the midst of the chaos. "What is your sign?"

"Pisces!"

"Me too," she says in delight, "and your ascendant, have you calculated it?"

I show her my white paper. "Not yet."

Paris, September 1989

Once again I am a newborn on the second floor of a brothel and I have uttered my first cry at 3 a.m. My mother has left me on the platform of a station, a November morning when it was very cold. She died at Riga on August 20, 1944 with my brother who had managed to grow up to age twelve. The Russian army was at the gates of the ghetto, an SS officer wanted to give himself the pleasure of one last "present" I was told by Hilde Sherman who witnessed the scene. In the forest, on the edge of a trench they had to strip, both of them. Gerd was thin and undersized. Mommy hid her breasts and her pubic area like any humiliated woman. They fell back into the trench, a dull thud, scarcely perceptible, the other bodies muffled the impact. My trip to Mönchengladbach had made me go back to the sources of my life, to that "void" that the strange little bookseller in the gray smock had discovered in the "map of my heavens."

In my native town, today a large opulent city, I felt lonely. Lonely even with my little adopted mother who told me her schoolgirl memories to dry my eyes which were full, even during the night.

Here, we were both alone, alone in a way to make us die of sorrow, in the midst of a crowd of little old men, little old women, and the ghosts of six million dead. At night in my bed and during the day in the streets, I groped in the emptiness for the reassuring hand that Maxime had once put on mine, one June evening of 1964 in the Ambigu Theater's book and stationery shop.

P.S. I sent a postcard to Tania, a beautiful one in colors of the Champs de Mars with Dutch tulips in bloom.

"The Eiffel Tower says hello."

I signed it "Your friend Pisces-Sagittarius, the sign of fire."

Caroline Alexander, journalist and drama critic, was born in the Rhineland where Jewish communities had existed for more than a thousand years. The infamous Nazi chapter in Germany's history compelled many to flee: three-year-old Ingeborg-Karoline was smuggled out at the last moment and so escaped the fate of millions of others.

A German Chronology...

30 January 1933	Hitler becomes Chancellor of the Reich. Subsequent boycott of Jewish shops. "Aryanization" of the civil service.
15 September 1935	The Nuremberg Racial Laws "For the Protection of German Blood and Honor" (*zum Schutz Deutschen Blutes und Deutscher Ehre*).
25 February 1936	Birth in Mönchengladbach (Rhineland) of Ingeborg-Karoline.
17 August 1938	A new law stipulates that all Jewish females must be registered under the first name of Sara and males under the name of Israel.
9-10 November 1938	The so-called *Kristallnacht* (night of broken glass), a party and state-orchestrated pogrom against Jews all over Germany. Some 117 synagogues set on fire and gutted; 20,000 Jewish men arrested and sent to prisons and concentration camps.

2 September 1939	Invasion of Poland. Beginning of World War II.
10 November 1939	Ingeborg-Karoline spirited out of Germany to Belgium.
31 July 1941	Göring empowers Heydrich to proceed with the mass-deportation to Russia of all Jews in German-held territories. It was the official beginning of the "Final Solution of the Jewish question."
20 January 1942	Wannsee Conference, further organizing the "Final Solution."
1946	Nuremberg Tribunal on war crimes reveal numbers murdered in the Holocaust: 6,000,000 Jews among which were 1,800,000 children.
16 February 1948	The law on Jewish first names is finally declared null and void.
August 1989	The city of Mönchengladbach hosts some 164 Shoah (Holocaust) survivors and their companions.

About the Author

For more than thirty years Caroline Alexander has lived in Paris. She has been a professional journalist since 1969.

As a young woman she studied law for two years at the University of Brussels, but her passion for the arts and especially the theatre brought her to Paris around 1958. There she studied dramatic art, and worked for five years as an actress. Her career as a journalist and writer began in 1966 when she started the first cultural columns for *Femme Pratique* and *Femmes D'Aujourd'Hui*, two popular women's magazines.

Alexander is the author of *Ma Vie de Branquignot*, a biography of the director Robert Dhery. She adapted from German into French Arthur Schnitzler's drama *Zwischenspiel* (Interlude) and *Fink und Fliederbusch "Les Journalistes–Merle et Mimosas"* both published by Actes–Sud Papiers. *Les Journalistes* will be produced in May 1994 at the Théâtre National de la Colline.

Alexander spent three years in London covering cultural events for *Le Matin* and for *La Vie Francaise*. She speaks French, English and German and has some knowledge of Dutch and Spanish.

During her ten years at *L'Express* she covered many areas of the arts, especially theatre, both in France and during regular visits to Great Britain. When Caroline Alexander left *L'Express* in 1979, she joined *Paris–Hebdo's* journalistic team. Until 1984 she was television, music and opera critic of the daily financial newspaper *Les Echos*.

Over the years her work has appeared in many French and Belgian publications. She is currently theatre and music critic at *La Tribune Desfosses*, the other main daily economic newspaper of France. Her voice has become known to many through her broadcasts on the "France-Inter," "France-Culture" and "France-Musique" radio networks. As a drama and music critic, she is a former vice-president of the "Syndicat de la Critique Dramatique et Musicale" and an active member of the "International Association of Theatre Critics."

She loves opera, painting, poetry, (classic as well as avant-garde), cats, dogs and horses. Married with two children, a girl and a boy–both actors–, she writes articles, plays and novels among her cats in a large house full of flowers.

The typeface used in this book is Goudy. It is a classic old style type; modeled on the humanist bookhand for lowercase letters and Roman capitals for the uppercase letters. It was designed in 1915 by the American Frederic Goudy, the world's first full-time type designer.

PRINTED IN CANADA